SUPER ADVANCED APP MARKETING

From The Youngest App Marketing Expert In the World.

———

(Author - Abhinav Ojha)

SUPER ADVANCED APP MARKETING

Copyright © 2021 by Abhinav Ojha

All rights reserved. No part of this book may be reproduced or transmitted in any form or by any means without written permission from the author.

Disclaimer

Although the author and publisher have made every effort to ensure that the information in this book was correct at press time, the author and publisher do not assume and hereby disclaim any liability to any party for any loss, damage, or disruption caused by errors or omissions, whether such errors or omissions result from negligence, accident, or any other cause.

Email: dabhinavojha@gmail.com

Website : www.abhinavojha.com

Facebook: www.facebook.com/abhinavojhaa

Table of Contents

Foreword 6

Before we Start 7

How everything began for me 9

Getting Laid Off 14

Chapter 1 7

Chapter 2 21

Chapter 3 37

Chapter 4 71

Chapter 5 93

Chapter 6 101

Chapter 7 113

Chapter 8 233

Chapter 9 247

Chapter 10 261

Chapter 11 281

Chapter 12 293

Chapter 13 7

Chapter 14 21

Chapter 15.. 37

Chapter 16.. 71

Chapter 17 93

Chapter 18 101

Chapter 19 113

Chapter 20 233

Chapter 21 247

Chapter 22 261

Chapter 23 281

Chapter 24 293

Chapter 25 233

Forewood

I wrote this book with empathy for your excursion as an entrepreneur, developer, blogger, writer, and an engineering student. If you are simply beginning your business, I understand that it is so hard to succeed. I was additionally at a similar spot where you are at the present time and I have encountered the pressure and stress you are feeling myself. The fundamental objective of this book is to shorten the time of struggle and provide all in one guide to succeed in the Mobile App business.

The guide and exhortation in this book depend on my own experience. I began my Mobile application business being a developer myself with only $10 in my hand and figured out how to get lakhs of downloads for myself as well as my clients in a short span of time.

I wish you the best of luck and hope that this book will add to your success.

Before We Start

I value you placing confidence and time in my work by perusing this book and I don't take that for granted. While writing this book, I attempted my best to cover each and everything that may add to your success and assist you with developing in the Mobile application business. I have canvassed everything in this book that will assist you in developing your business to its fullest potential from development to marketing.

My own email address - dabhinavojha@gmail.com

My Facebook page   - https://www.facebook.com/abhinavojhaa

Who Am I?

Hello everyone, I am Abhinav Ojha ,one of the youngest App Marketing and ASO experts in the World .You can search about me on google .Currently I am the Founder and CEO of Enterstor Pvt Ltd.

How Everything Began For Me

In early 2017, I was experiencing watching videos and perusing articles for beginning a tech blog. Following one month of increasing every one of that information on the best way to begin a blog, I at long last started a tech blog named Trending Techies in May 2017. This was the start of my entrance into the digital world.

I was so enthusiastic about innovation from my youth days. I had incredible energy and desire for learning new things and advances. In August 2017, I took admission in an engineering college known as Jis college of engineering, Kalyani. I took admission in the subject of information technology that was my childhood passion so I chose to follow my passion with extraordinary assurance.

Towards the end of 2017, I had expounded on 70 articles on my blog with one sponsored article from top-passwords.com that was about how to recover a lost password using that product. I got $30 for writing that sponsored article and I was so upbeat since that was my first salary.I soon utilized that amount in digital marketing running google ads campaign and using online marketing methods to promote my blog.

Anyway, I was not all that accomplished in digital marketing then, the amount that I earned was pretty much squandered in advancing my blog since I had no clue about keywords, running campaigns, CPC, etc. However, I gained from my failures and didn't rehash similar missteps next time.

Meanwhile, I was gaining extraordinary information on SEO that is search engine optimization while running my blog, I got acquainted with techniques to rank blog, backlinks,off-page, and on-page search engine optimization thus on. Soon I chose to launch a digital ebook on amazon kindle to help people start their own blog without much effort and investments.

At the June end of 2018, I had just written two digital ebooks that were distributed on amazon kindle. One was about beginner's guide to starting a blog without investment which I mentioned earlier and the other was a basic guide to ethical hacking.

The ebook beginners guide to start a blog comprised of every one of those pieces of information that a beginner should know before starting a blog. The ebook was essentially focused on beginning a blog on the blogger platform without much investment. It has all information from setting up a custom domain name, indexing pages on google search console, get google AdSense account approved for monetization, use analytics, etc.

Anyway barely any months prior to the consummation of 2018, something happened that constrained me to leave blogging for not many months, I was gaining a lot of information about strategies to make a blog successful. I had just positioned 3 to 4 articles of my blog on Google's first page till then. But getting inspired by some ace bloggers I chose to take my blog to another level and the primary thing that I needed to change in my blog was the domain name. I needed to include some high traffic keywords for my domain name and migrate my blog to WordPress from blogger for additional exposure and complete rights facilitating my blog by self. Wordpress is one of the best CMS for running blogs since 69% of websites including blogs are powered by WordPress.We get the help of lot of plugins in WordPress to make our task easier. But I did some specialized missteps while moving my blog from Blogger to Wordpress and the redirection didn't function well and finally, I lost all the rankings of my blog. That was truly disappointing for me. I left writing articles from that point forward in light of the fact that I was propelled however I adapted such a large number of strategies of the ranking blog, getting AdSense approval, digital marketing procedures, etc which I took emphatically and proceeded onward.

Subsequent to getting demotivated from blogging toward the finish of 2018, I was progressively centered around developing android applications than running blogs since I was a generally excellent developer from my youth days itself yet the enthusiasm for learning digital marketing continued. I used to help my friends, relatives, and so forth to advance their items and business online through digital marketing. I had viewed around a large number of youtube videos and articles about promoting online till that time.

I began developing android applications with incredible enthusiasm and vitality. However, I already had 1 year of experience in developing apps until then.

Getting Laid Off

It was March 2019, and I would consider it as a defining moment in my life. Our college, Jis College of Engineering organized a tech-fest which was known as Jistech 2k19 and there were a lot of competitions organized for students. What's more, one of them was App E Teaser for application development and I was chosen the winner of APP_E_Teaser for developing eCommerce android application and the strategies for advertising that android application was considered as amazing by the board of judges. I was given the honor of Jisce APP star where all the engineering colleges of West Bengal, India took an interest in that competition. The measure of certainty and gratefulness I received gave me a great deal of joy and my certainty was helped to another level. Soon then I chose to take my application development career to an unheard-of level..

It was May 2019, I uploaded my first android application on google play store. Till the end of August, I added 5 more applications on google play store taking the aggregate to 6. I applied all my Digital marketing and internet advertising procedures to advance my application store. Meanwhile, I likewise worked for five organizations as an intern for various job roles such as developer, sales expert, digital marketer, and so forth that uncovered me more and gave me more experiences. Till the end of December, I had just propelled 15 applications on google play store and inside 5 months I got the recipe for positioning the android applications on google play store. I for the most part created applications by utilizing keywords that are I created applications on keywords that have high traffic and search volume, for example, Love Quotes. Love quotes are a keyword that is being looked through more than 1 million times in one month. So creating applications on high hunt volume keywords will definitely give us higher installs. Currently, I have 20+ applications accessible on google play store and 90% of the applications are positioned in the top 10 of google play store rankings. I finished my initial 1 lakh downloads on my applications inside 4 months without contributing much on marketing and with no subsidizing help since I was a 3rrd year IT understudy that time, I just had restricted add up to spend on promoting, in a matter of time I arrived at 500k downloads all alone applications inside a half year spending just 20000 INR (Indian rupees) for advertising that is around the US $300 only. This was awesome. Soon I began taking clients and helped their applications to get positioned in the top 10 of google play store rankings. Digital Marketing combined with the right ASO strategies will give you massive results.

In the meantime from August 2019 to December 2019 I was also working as an intern in top companies as I referenced before where I helped them in deals through digital marketing and the gratefulness I received from them was colossal.

Before long I explored all the strategies for rankings android applications in the top 10 in google play store and furthermore helped a large number of my customers and furthermore companions to advertise their apps. Some of my companions were noncoders too. They used to create applications from online tools, for example, thunkable and kodular and they had no capacities or extraordinary highlights in their applications yet at the same time, they used to get positioned at the top 10 by utilizing the right strategies of digital marketing and ASO. I helped parcel of them make at least $200 from their applications without knowing coding abilities.

Before long I began taking increasingly more digital marketing ventures from every one of my customers and conveyed 90% achievement rate to them.

As of now, I am making thousands of dollars just from my applications on google play store in the third year of my engineering. And I additionally take up customers' ventures and help their application positioned in the top 10 of google play store rankings. And to your surprise, I am only 21 years of age. Till now I have helped more than 50+ clients to achieve their goals in the field of app development.

This is the manner in which I began with application development and marketing.

Lets Explore.

WHY YOU SHOULD READ THIS BOOK.

This book is particularly written for single developers(without a team and funding support) who make a solid effort to build up their applications yet tragically couldn't receive many downloads on their applications and couldn't bring in money from it. This book covers 20+ ASO that is App Store Optimization strategies alongside a few internet and online-based marketing procedures and digital marketing that will assist the developers with getting increasingly more downloads on their applications and at last, can bring in money from their apps. This book will assist them with each progression from uploading applications to advancing and marketing, to spare marketing cost, maximize their incomes thus on. There are just 3 to 4 % of developers who arrive at 100k downloads on google play store. the details are taken from a survey. By perusing this book one can without much of a stretch adjust right ASO methods alongside digital marketing and achieve their objectives and goals and competitive single-handedly in the market.

Chapter One
Why We Need A Mobile App Business in 2020.

The use of mobile apps either an android application or an ios application is expanding step by step and with the simple access to the web and internet and increment in mobile devices, it will proceed to develop and become significantly more in the future. There is at present 3.5 billion smartphones all-inclusive in 2020, while it was 3.2 billion in 2019. The number of smartphone users is expanding day by day, in that situation having a mobile application business is a fantastic idea. Global cell phone users have increment by 40% from the year 2016 and are probably going to build increasingly more in the coming years. According to a report, cell phone users will reach 7.5 billion continuously in 2023. By 2025, 72% of all web users will exclusively utilize cell phones to get to the web. Subsequently, you should attempt to explore the mobile application business that will increase gigantic potential in the up and coming years. Here I have come up with certain insights 0f mobile apps.

1. Desktop internet usage is falling & mobile internet usage is rising.

Individuals are investing more energy and time in mobile devices instead of on the desktop. Even the blogs and sites are seen more on mobile phones than on desktop computers and will impressively fall in the up and coming years.

2. Users downloaded 178 billion apps in 2017

As per ongoing statistics, users have downloaded in excess of 178 billion apps globally in the year 2017. You can without much of a stretch notice the capability of mobile apps in the up and coming years. That number is projected to grow to 205 billion this year, and 258 billion in 2022—a 45 percent increase over five years.

3. Mobile apps are anticipated to hit $188.9 billion in revenue by 2020.

There is a 113% expansion in mobile application incomes in the previous four years and will continue to ascend in forthcoming years moreover.

4. Mobile users are investing 87 percent of their energy and time in apps, versus only 13 percent on the web.

In 2017, cell phone and tablet users invested 87 percent of their energy in apps. This implies that for consistently spent on the web, users were going through almost seven hours utilizing mobile apps.

5.Percentage of most utilized mobile apps

1.Social Media Apps - 39%

2.Gaming Apps - 10%

3.Communication and chat apps - 10%

4. Retail Apps - 7%

5. Other Apps - 34%

5. Key Mobile App Insights

- Mobile apps will produce $189 billion in income by 2020.

- The Apple Application Store has 2.2 million apps accessible for download.

- There are 2.8 million apps accessible for download on the Google Play Store.

- 21% of Recent college grads open an application 50+ times each day.

- 49% of individuals open an application 11+ occasions every day.

- 57% of every digital media use originates from mobile apps.

- The normal cell phone proprietor utilizes 30 apps every month.

- Specialists foresee that there will be a 25% expansion in worldwide application downloads somewhere in the range of 2018 and 2022.

- A year ago, there were in excess of 205 billion application downloads. That's a 15% expansion from the year earlier.

- 98% of application income overall originates from free apps. Only a small amount of individuals are eager to pay for downloads.

- According to a recent research,83% of shoppers use shopping apps.

- About 58% of users said Social, Gaming, and Communication were their best three most utilized application categories.

- Application categories with use underneath 4% – Internet business, Travel, Maps, Account among others – were utilized on a need-premise.

- About 75% of respondents affirmed that the main 5 application classes are the ones they connect with regularly.

- Absolute time spent on mobile devices every day: 215 minutes, or three hours and 35 minutes. It's required to arrive at three hours and 49 minutes by 2020.

- Time spent on mobile sites? 13 minutes per day, as indicated by eMarketer. By 2020, that will probably drop to 12 minutes every day.

- By 2022 application store shopper spending is anticipated to increment by 92 percent to $157 billion around the world

- Mobile application users in the US have more than 100 apps introduced on their cell phones

- The normal mobile user checks their cell phone 63 times each day

- 87 percent of users will check their smartphones at any rate one hour before rest, and 69 percent of those users will check their phones inside 5 minutes before rest.

- The most popular form of app store optimization (ASO) came in the form of description updates at 46 percent

- App icon updates were the second most frequent form of ASO at 30 percent, up 24 percent year over year.

- 34 Percent of marketers hope to have a voice application by 2020

- 83% of enterprise workloads will be in the cloud by 2020.

When and where are people using mobile devices?

- 93% at home
- 85% while in the washroom
- 75% while having dinner
- 72% at work
- 79% when with family/friends
- 74% waiting in lines of waiting for appointments
- 65% while shopping
- 79% while watching TV
- 65% during the commute to work
- 79% during miscellaneous downtime throughout the day

Chapter Two

The most effective method to Develop Apps.

There are a number of ways you can get your application developed or develop it yourself.

1. Develop your application by Yourself.

2. Hire a Freelancer to get your application created.

3. Contact Mobile application organizations to build up your application.

4. Partner with developers on an offer premise or percentage shares to build up your apps.

5. Use online free tools to create an app. (Not Recommended).

You can develop your app by yourself if you are a good programmer or developer. However, creating complex apps can be tedious and can require a parcel of involvement with mobile application development. If you can build up your application by yourself, you are going to spare your development cost without a doubt.

You can either hire a freelancer online and get your project done. Most people hire freelancers these days for the development of their projects.

You can likewise contact the top and best mobile application development companies to build up your apps.

You can partner with other developers and get your project developed on a share basis that means you have to appoint that developer as a co-founder of your startup and have to give a percentage of share to him/her.

There are a lot of online tools for developing apps.You can also use any of them if the project is simple and easy.However using online tools to develop apps is not at all recommended as it has so many disadvantages and is never suggested for long-term mobile app business.

Note - Please make sure to have a legal agreement ,if you are getting your app developed from someone else such as an app development company or other developers including freelancers so that you won't face any security issues in the future and your data would not be stolen by anyone of them.Make a legal agreement with both you and the developer enlisting all the details and features of your project and a bond that your app should not be reused in any way on any platform or any of the data should not be stolen in future.

Chapter Three

Gettng started

Brief guide to Google play console dashboard

DASHBOARD

Here you will get all the pieces of information about your application, for example, how the KPIs are performing.KPI represents key execution indicators. You will likewise get details of the retention rate of your application, for example, how much users have installed the application and the amount of them have uninstalled it and how much active devices the application is at present introduced into. Along with that, you will get reports of ratings and reviews of your application and crash reports. You will likewise discover reports of your audience growth and countries your application is introduced into.

STATISTICS

Here you will get all the details of your applications from ratings and reviews to audience, android devices your application is introduced into, date range, and so on, etc.

ANDROID VITALS

These will have four sub-classifications, for example, overview.crashes and ANR, App size and deobfuscation records.

DEVELOPMENT TOOLS

This classification has two sub-classification, for example, internal application sharing and Services and API's, this interface segment comprises of the API's you are using.

RELEASE MANAGEMENT

Here you will deal with your application from uploading your application to production, beta version, updating your apps. It has a few subclasses, for example, Release dashboard, App releases which will comprise all the adaptations of applications you have released, Android instant apps, Artifact library, Device catalog. App signing and pre-launch report.

STORE PRESENCE - This is the principle region we use for ASO that is App Store Optimisation. We will examine it in detail later. It has a few subclasses, for example, Store listing, experiments, custom store listings, pricing and distribution of your app, content rating, app content, and in-application items in the event that you have alongside translation services.

USER ACQUISITION -

Here you will get all acquisition reports, google advertisements campaigns, promotions, and improvement tips.

USER FEEDBACK - Here you will get all the data about your application reviews, ratings, review analysis, and beta feedback.

*Note - Only the significant focuses are talked about in this section that is significant for ASO (App Store Optimization).

Chapter Four
What is App Store Optimization.

ASO represents App Store Optimization the same as SEO that is Search Engine Optimisation.SEO helps in positioning your site or websites or blogs in Google search results known as SERP. There are two sorts of SEO methods i.e off-page search engine optimization and on-page SEO. However, we won't talk much about SEO in this book. However, I have clarified about SEO in detail later in this book.ASO in short can be characterized as the way toward improving application visibility inside application stores, for example, apple store or google play store and expanding conversion rates that are organic downloads.ASO likewise centers around Click Through Rate (CTR). This implies you need to persuade individuals to really click into your application store listing once they discover it. Higher the visibility, more the downloads. You can do as such by advancing your App Name, App Title, App Icon, App Screenshots, and App Rating and reviews and playing with keywords wisely..So ASO like SEO encourages us in ranking our applications on google play store or apple app store rankings. App developers or organizations must utilize

ASO techniques to get their applications ranked higher on google play store and at last get higher organic installs.

When individuals navigate to your application store listing page, you need to ensure they additionally download it or make a buy. This piece of ASO is otherwise called Conversion Rate Optimization (CRO).

The calculation for ranking applications isn't known to anybody, only google knows how they rank applications on google play store and same applies to apple application store as well however that is not the point to stress, if the methods would not be known to anybody, I wouldn't write this book. It's genuine that even I don't the method for ranking applications yet yes I have the experience of positioning 90% of my applications in top 10 in google play store search results, I have additionally ranked huge numbers of, my customer's apps, companies I worked for, etc in top 10 of google play store rankings. If right ASO methods are utilized you can without much of a stretch rank your applications on play store with appropriate streamlining strategies joined with keyword research and in particular Digital marketing. There are over 3.6 million android applications on google play store and about 2.7 million applications on apple store. How it's feasible for your application to hang out in that extreme competition. That is the reason ASO is utilized. Developing an application isn't an issue, marketing is. There is hellfire parcel of applications advanced with such a large amount of features still doesn't have downloads considerably more than 100. This is where digital marketing is utilized along with a legitimate app store optimization strategy.

Quick difference between ASO and SEO.

ASO is regularly alluded to as app store SEO (Search Engine Optimization). The two procedures share likenesses like keyword optimizations, backlinks and conversion enhancement. The fundamental contrasts between App Store Optimization and Search Engine Optimization are the ranking elements. Additionally, ASO is used for mobile applications while SEO is for sites and blogs.

SEO factors for an internet browser, similar to Google Search, include in excess of 200 viewpoints and the rundown continues growing. The rundown of ranking components for ASO is a lot shorter, anyway numerous individuals are as yet uncertain of which ones play a major role.Reading this book is an ideal opportunity to stop that!. I have mentioned around 20+ ASO strategies in this book to boost your app ranking within 15 days.

Before we move on to optimization strategies and techniques let me tell you that there are basically two types of ASO.

1. On page ASO - On page ASO includes all those techniques and strategies mentioned in the next chapter.

2.Off-page ASO - Off-page ASO is hidden factors that determine app rankings and these factors are unrevealed by google or apple. These are some special and hidden factors that add value to apps rankings.

Here are some of the most common ASO techniques used for ranking your apps on google play store or apple store.

1. Proper Icon

2.Package name

3..A good and descriptive titles including some keywords.

4. Keyword Research

5...A good short description

6...A proper full description playing with keywords well and targeting keywords.

7...Managing tags and categories

8...Awesome screenshots of your app.

9...A well edited promo video.

10.. Positive Reviews and ratings

11. Users retained

12. App size

13. Share App option

14. App Store Analytics

15. Tracking/Monitoring main KPI's.

16. App Updates

17. Backlinks and Landing page

18. Replying to all the reviews.

19. App Engagement

20. Conversion

21. Hidden and Special Factors

Chapter Five

White Hat, Black Hat and Grey Hat ASO

White Hat ASO - White hat ASO alludes to any practice that improves your applications search performance on an App store listing which is known as APL while keeping up the respectability of the application and remaining inside the guidelines, terms, and conditions of the google play store or apple store. It predominantly incorporates the utilization of genuine optimization techniques and strategies that improves your application rankings. White Hat ASO procedures never violate any policies and are working on following terms and conditions and remaining inside the rules.

Black Hat ASO - Black Hat ASO is inverse or opposite to white Hat ASO. It includes accomplishing something that disregards or violates google play or apple store policies and getting downloads that aren't legit. This includes fraudulent activities performed by developers to get their application positioned and get more installs. This hack can, at last, suspend or ban your application or even suspend your developer's account permanently since its not legit. Some instances of Black Hat ASO incorporates counterfeit downloads, fake ratings and reviews, and rehearsing fraudulent activities. Using non-genuine approaches to improve rankings, getting downloads etc goes under Black Hat ASO.

Grey Hat ASO - Gray Hat ASO is a mixture or combination of both White Hat ASO and Black Hat ASO. Most regular practices incorporate purchasing application downloads, app reviews, reskinning applications that is utilizing others application with your own name and package name, etc.Copying others content, etc.

Chapter Six

ASO Strategies in detail.

1. Proper Icon -

This is one of the most significant procedure for ASO. An all-around made attractive icon draws in users and eventually expands CTR that represents Click-Through Rate. In this case, CTR can be characterized as the no of clicks your application receives partitioned by no of impressions.

CTR(Click Through Rate)=Clicks/impressions*100.

If your application receives 10 clicks and absolute impressions are 100 that your CTR is 10/100*100 i.e 10%.Most probably users will generally click more on the initial 10 applications listed and there an attractive icon can assist you with getting more CTR and that will wind up having more installs to your application.

The suggested colors you can use for your application icons are red, blue, black, pink, and orange, and green. These hues will draw in users to tap on your app more than other colors. Dark colors can have higher CTR than light colors. Try to make your application icon as appealing and attractive as possible.

Pro Tip -

1. Recommended colors are red, blue, black, pink, orange, and green. Any mix will likewise work.

2. Use keywords in icon names while uploading an icon to the application stores. For example use, the icon name as keyword.png and afterward upload it on application stores.

3. You can also update your icon regurarly making some minor changes as it contributes to 30% in App store Optimization.Stats taken from recent reports.

2.Package name -

The package name of our application is likewise essential for ASO. Attempt to keep the package name the same as the application name /title of application that may help you in the ranking of your app. Many of us simply overlook the package name yet these little seemingly insignificant details make a significant difference in the ranking of your app. You can likewise focus on certain keywords in your package name the same as your application name.

Example for package name - com.lovequotes.cutelovequotes.

Regardless of whether you are building up your application or getting it developed from somebody else, please make sure that you use certain keywords in the package name too. The package name is something nobody makes a fuss over however can truly help in ranking applications to an extent.

Pro tip - Use at least two keywords, one main keyword, and one supporting keyword in the package name of your application.

3. Descriptive and catchy title including keywords

Apple application store gives 30 characters to your title while google play store gives just 50 characters yet you get a short description of 80 characters on google play store. You must incorporate keywords that you need to get ranked for in your application title. For instance, you need to publish an application for Love quotes, so ensure the keyword love quotes are present in the title and furthermore in the package name as mentioned earlier. With love quotes as your main keyword, you can likewise use supporting keywords, for example, cute love quotes, love quotes for her thus on.(Keyword research is clarified in subtleties later in this book).You should use at least 2 keywords in your application titles i.e one primary keyword and one supporting keyword in a legitimate way that draws in users and is appealing to the eyes. and unique at the same time.

Here is the example for the title - Love Quotes| Cute love quotes, Love Poems, Valentine Quotes

Including keywords for both the package name and title can help your application rankings by 200%. So make a point to utilize keywords in an appropriate way. That is one of the most crucial strategies for App Store Optimisation. The same represents for a short description as well,try to play with keywords in the short description too. You can likewise utilize title with captions focusing on keywords. Make sure the title of your application is easy to read, unique, and catchy.

Pro tips -

1. Avoid conjunctions and prepositions.

2. Don't use numbers in the title of your application.

3. Separate title by using , or |.

4. Include one primary keyword and one supporting keyword at least in the title.

5. The title ought to be unique and simple to read.

6. The title should be Relevant to the App.

4. Keyword Research -

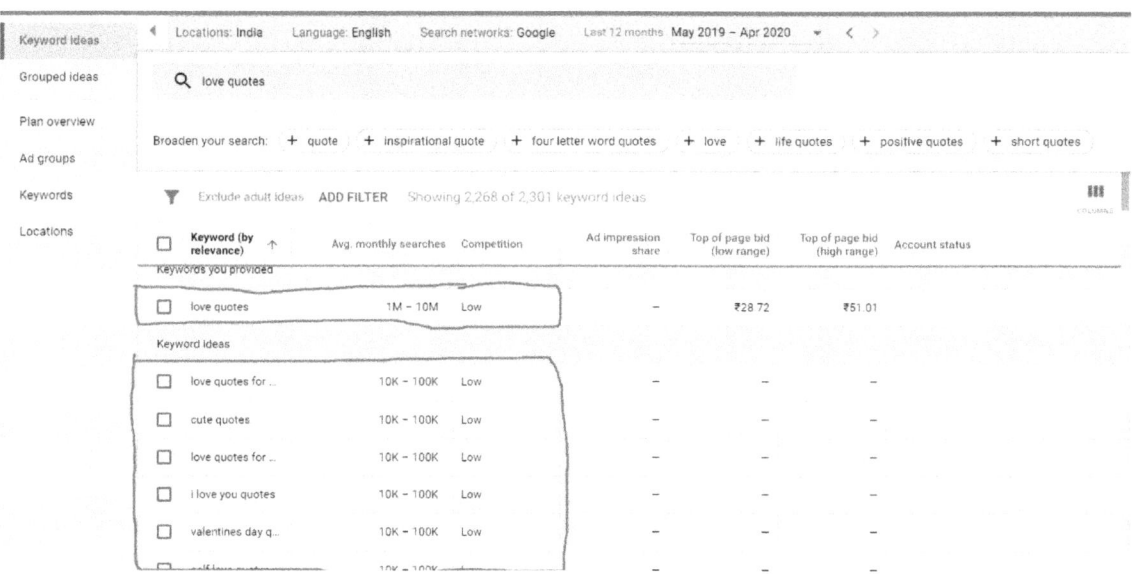

A keyword can be described as a word or phrase that individuals use to look at applications either in google play store or apple application store. The above screenShot is taken from google Ads keyword planner tool which is one of the most remarkable keywords planners and simultaneously free as well. Here in the above screenshot, you can see the search volume of the keywords love quotes. It has been looked through 1M to 10M times normal in a month in search results and the competition is quite low for this keyword. Competition implies less no of contenders are working for this keyword. Lower the Competition, higher the possibility of getting your applications positioned in google play store or App store and furthermore higher the search volume, higher the possibility of getting more traffic to your application or installs. Along with that in the event that you can discover beneath, there is parcel of supporting keywords excessively, for example, love quotes for her, cute quotes, I love you quotes, valentines day quotes thus on. These keywords can be utilized as supporting keywords with your principle keyword which is love quotes. By utilizing google keywords planner you can investigate each one of those keywords and target it in your App store for doing ASO (App Store Optimisation) and ranking your app.However this was only a short prologue to keyword research, we will be realizing it in subtleties later in this book and furthermore about best tools for keywords research and some low competition keywords, Page bids, the low and high range and each different things in subtleties in next section.

AppRadar, MobileDevHq, and TheTool, Google keyword planner are probably the most useful assets for App store Optimisations that will locate some best App store keywords for your application.

Pro Tips -

1. Try to include the primary keyword in your application title or package name as referenced before.

2. Try to use words rather than phrases.

3. Avoid conjunctions and prepositions

4. Use commas or | for isolating keywords

5. Use digits rather than spellings.

In apple application store you get just 100 characters for your application description so you need to play with keywords all the more astutely while in google play store you get 4000 characters for your application full description.

5. A good short description -

As mentioned earlier try to include two keywords in your apps short description, it can be one main keyword and one supporting keyword same as app title.

Pro tips - Keep it simple and unique.

6. A proper full description -

In the Apple application store, you get just 100 characters for description so you need to play admirably with your keywords, don't target something that's not required while in google play store you get 4000 characters for providing your applications description in detail.

The App Description is another fundamental piece of your application's metadata. It furnishes users with data on what your application is about and gives a review of its principle highlights.

The App Description isn't just applicable for the users, yet additionally for the application stores' ranking factors too.

It's particularly significant for Google Play. The description is one of the primary areas where Google finds the keywords to rank your application. This doesn't mean you can simply place every one of your keywords into description and trust that the ranking will occur. Attempt to consolidate your keywords into sentences normally and naturally.

Apple won't file keywords from your iOS application description like Google play. That doesn't mean you ought to disregard this metadata field. You can in any case use it as a chance to additionally show individuals the advantages and estimation of your application.

In short, your description should be simple, easy, and straightforward.

You can utilize the underneath technique for your description in google play store.

*Introduction

*Full Description

*Tags

*Disclaimer if necessary.

In the introduction, part try to give a concise description of your application and focusing on keywords.

In full description part , write full description simply like you compose articles yet with focusing on fundamental keywords and supporting keywords and furthermore ensure don't overuse any keywords, you can focus on a keyword greatest multiple times in your full description. Try to target a keyword minimum two times and a maximum of four and not more than that. Over doing it might bring down your application rankings and may affect ASO negatively. So ensure you target one keyword to a limit of multiple times maximum four in particular. You can target supporting keywords joined with them as expressed before.

Pro Tips -

- *Informative
- *straightforward
- *Obviously organized with bullet points and emojis.
- *Targetting keywords (particularly with Google Play)
- *Up to 4000 characters in length
- *Pay extra attention to Full description as it accounts to 46% contribution in ASO.

And also try to describe your app well in this section such as -

1. What does your app do?
2. What are its features?
3. What problems it can solve?
4. Why users should install this app?

Example - Here in the example your main keyword is love quotes so don't use love quotes more than 4 times in your description and same applies to supporting keywords such as cute love quotes etc.

Tags - This is also one of the most important parts of your description and also ASO. You have to use it very wisely. You can use this for google play store only since the apple store provides only 100 characters for description but you can surely use it for android apps in the google play store since it provides 4000 characters. So in the tags section use one keyword one time only, don't repeat a single keyword twice because it may violate google play store policies.

Example of using tags -

You can also find some more features in our app listed below -

1.Love quotes 2020

2.Best love quotes

3.Cute love Quotes

4.Anniversory love quotes

Disclaimer part is optional you can have it or neglect it.

7. Managing tags and categories -

Use those tags and categories that best suits your app .Don't use the category that is not at all related to your app.Make sure to select relevant category for your apps.

Here are some pro tips to focus on while choosing category for your app -

    1.   Try to choose relevant category for your app that best suits your app.

    2.   Choosing a less competitive category can higher the rankings of your app.Choose a category that is less competitive i.e less apps are available for that category.

8. Awesome and Attractive Screenshots -

According to a survey people spend only 7 seconds deciding whether they are going to download your app or not. So it's very important to make your store page look as attractive as possible and attractive well-designed screenshots play a major role in making your store look beautiful. They are considered as the second most influential factor after app ratings for convincing someone to download your apps.

Some of the top free online tools to design beautiful screenshots.

- App Screenshot Builder by Applaunchpad.
- App Screenshot Maker by AppInstitute.
- ShotBot.
- Davinci Apps.
- App Store Screenshot.
- Appure.
- StoreShots.
- PlaceIt.

Pro Tip -

Try to show your main features of your apps in screenshots and design screenshot for mobiles, tablets, portrait screenshots and landscape screenshots.

Adding keywords in name of screenshots will boost your app rankings to atmost 30%. Try to add keywords in your screenshots name before uploading it to app stores.

9. Promo Video -

Design a short attractive promo video that mainly focuses on showing the main features of your app. Don't waste precious seconds showing something that is not at all related to your app. An attractive promo video can increase the chances of getting your app installed.

Pro Tips -

1. You can create promo videos for your app from Renderforest for free.

2. Keep the duration of promo video as minimum as possible.

10. Positive reviews and ratings -

Positive reviews and ratings play a vital role in getting more installs and also for getting higher rankings. People tend to download and trust those apps only which has good ratings and reviews. Try to get as many good positive reviews as possible.

Pro tips -

1. Get at least 50 paid reviews just after launching your app. Paid reviews can increase the chances of getting your app ranked. However most of the experts don't encourage this but according to my experience, it can help you get your app ranked to a great extent. It's very difficult to get genuine and positive reviews just after your app launch. You can go for 40 to 50 paid reviews only and not more than that. You can also tell your friends and family to review your app.

2. Use cloud messaging service to send notifications to the users of your apps to review your app and rate you 5 stars if they are liking your app.

3. Use a pop up asking users to review and rate your app.

4. Place a rate us option inside your app either in the bottom navigation or in the navigation menu that depends upon the UI of your app. Very fewer people tend to go to store and rate your app even if they genuinely liked your app so it's better to place a rate us option inside your app.

11. Users retained -

Your app retention rate also plays a very major role in your app rankings. Retention rate can be defined as the no of users retained after installing your app. There are a lot of users who just uninstalls the app just after installing. Therefore its must that you pay attention to retaining users. You have to figure out best practices to retain as many users as you can. You can do this only by providing your users with great user experience. 30% retention rate is said to be a good retention rate that is 30 users are retained for 100 users installing your app.

Pro Tips -

Some pro tips for retaining users and improving your retention rate.

1. Your app should have an attractive UI/UX that will higher the chances of getting your users retained.

2. Your app should Provide some valuable features and functions and should be problem-solving.

3. App size - App size also plays a major role in retaining your users. Some users just uninstall larger size apps because of less storage so try to develop an app as lite as possible.

4. Free of bugs and crashes - No one likes to keep an app full of bugs and that crashes frequently. Your app should be bug-free and crash less and would provide users a awesome user experience.

12. App Size -

App size is the most important part of ASO and ranking. Apps that are less in size tend to get higher rankings in google play store and I completely agree with this statement based on my experience. Apps with less size will rank higher than apps with larger sizes. Also, lesser size app can help you retain your users. Try to avoid using unused codes in your apps that is not at all needed. Try to call images from a server rather than using it as a resource in your apps. Encourage best practices to make your app as lite as possible.

Some pro tips -

1. You can use the android app bundle if you are developing an android app using android studio.

2. Avoid unused codes.

3. Use images calling from a server rather than using it in your app's resources. Doing this may lower your app size.

4. Compress the size of images and other files.

13. Share App Option -

Many of the developers avoid putting share app option inside the app. Share app options can create a chain among users and can also make your app viral. Share app options can help your app move from one person to another based on likes and can bring in more and more organic installs that will finally boost your app rankings. There are very few users who will go to your app store page and share your app. Therefore keeping a share app option inside the app is most important.

Pro Tips -

1. Display a pop up to share app.

2. Use the share app option in bottom navigation.

3. Use share app option in navigation menu.

4.Can also use the share app option when the user is making a exit from your app.

14. **App store analytics -**

Same as google analytics for web marketing, there are a lot of mobile app analytics tools that will help you in marketing strategy. You will analyze your competition and work accordingly that will boost your rankings. These tools can give you extra exposure when it comes to analytics.

Here are some of the app analytics tools -

1.AppAnnie

2.Sensor Tower

3.App Brain

4.Appfigures

5.App rank Corner

6. Appstatics

7. Applique

8. Applyzer

9. Tune and etc.

15. **Tracking/Monitoring main KPI's-**

Track all KPI's, keywords, competitors, top charts. organic installs by country. Organic installs are those installs that you receive by organic search results. Also, check out for similar apps, conversion rates to install, revenues from installs, competitors updates and changes, and practices.

16. **App Updates -**

Updating your app frequently at least once in 30 days will increase the chances of getting your app ranked higher. So never leave an app without an update for 3 months or 6 months. Google play store or the app store will never rank apps that are outdated. Only the recently updated apps get higher rankings in stores. So try to update your app more frequently. Even if you are not providing some additional features, focus on making your app bug free and crash-free, and provide your users with recent updates.

Pro Tips -

1. Try to give updates for your app at least once a month.

2. You can give minor updates but should give updates frequently.

3. Try to make the app bug free.

17. **Landing page and backlinks -**

It's better to have an SEO (Search engine optimization) optimized webpage for our apps leaving a backlink to download our app. (Details about SEO is explained later in this book).The web page should be SEO optimized and should contain all the information about your app with screenshots and videos. By doing so we will be able to get downloads for our apps from google search results as well. We will discuss SEO in detail later in this book. You should also focus on getting backlinks to your apps from other blogs and websites. Backlinks mean someone on their website or blog is providing a link to your app describing something. Generating a lot of backlinks increases the chances of getting your app ranked.

Pro Tips -

1.Try to generate as many backlinks as possible.

2.Comment on forums and blogs with your app link or the landing page link.

3. Give answers on quora providing your app link or landing page link.

18.**Replying to all the reviews -**

Whether you get a positive review or a negative review for your app, its must that you reply to all those reviews, replying to reviews also has some importance for ranking your apps. Make sure you reply to all the reviews in a professional manner and assure the reviewers to fix all the issues they mentioned in the reviews.

Pro tips for replying -

Replying to a positive review -

Thanks for your valuable feedback. It really motivates us.

Replying to a negative review -

Sorry for the inconvenience caused. We are really working hard to make our app bug free and provide an amazing user experience.

19. App Engagement -

App engagement also plays a vital role in rankings. App engagement includes retention of users, reviews and ratings, and active devices. On how many devices your apps are active and frequently used.

20. Conversion -

The conversion rate also plays a major factor in your app rankings. Conversion rate can be defined as the no.of installs your app gets per no.of your app store listings.

Ex- conversion rate = no of installs/total no of app store impressions that users see.

In short, if your app store gets 100 impressions, then how many users end up installing your app after visiting your app store. If 10 users end up installing your app and your app store shows 100 impressions then your conversion rate is 10%.

21. Special factors -

There are also some special and hidden factors that google and apple will not tell anyone since its a hidden algorithm that no one knows. But following the above 20 strategies can 100% get your app ranked higher for sure.

ASO Quick Checklist.

1. ASO (APP Store Optimization) is very vital and important for getting your app ranked.

2. Full Description add to the highest ranking factors among all ASO factors.

3. App Icon plays a major role in increasing app"s CTR .

4. An well arranged attractive screenshots are the second most important factors to look after for optimizing your app store.

5. Adding tags in a right way can higher the chances of getting your app ranked.

6. Using all 4000 characters for providing full description in google play store will higher the chances of app ranking.

7. Adding keywords in name of screenshots and app icon can boost your app rankings by 30%.

8. Adding keywords in package name of your app can boost your app rankings to a great extent.

9. Developing keyword based apps will bring more and more downloads.

10.   ASO is still an ongoing process.

Chapter Seven

Some common google play violations made by developers

*We will discuss the common violated policies in brief.

1.Restricted Content

Child Endangerment

Inappropriate Content

Financial Services

Gambling

Illegal Activities

User Generated Content

Unapproved Substances

Using sexual content, inappropriate content, gambling, drugs, illegal activities, etc are strictly prohibited and should not be used in any way inside your app or you will find your app getting suspended.

2.Impersonation and Intellectual Property

Impersonation

Intellectual Property

Copying other's content or establishing a relationship with other brands in the wrong way is strictly prohibited. Copying others brand icon or using a brand name as a developer name which you are not authorized to do violates google play policies and will land your app in trouble for sure.

3. Privacy, Security, and Deception

User Data

Permissions

Device and Network Abuse

Malicious Behavior

Deceptive Behavior

Misrepresentation

Malware

If you violate any of the above-mentioned policies your app as well as your console account will be in trouble.

4. Store Listing and Promotion

App Promotion

Metadata

User Ratings, Reviews, and Installs

Content Ratings

This mainly includes using tags and descriptions in an improper way or using someone else icon or using any brand name in the title of your app etc. Using the correct content rating for your app is of utmost importance. Asking reviews from users providing them discounts and incentives is strictly prohibited and violated Google policies.

Chapter Eight

How to do keyword research using Google keyword planner.

Please note - Google Keyword Planner tool is 100% free to use. You need not spend a penny on AdWords ads to gain access. You just need a Google account.

In this chapter, I will show you how can you find some serious keywords that you may use for your apps using google keyword planner that's completely a free tool by google.

Let's get started.

Firstly you need to set up your google ads account and run some ads before getting access to google keyword planner but here in this chapter, I will show you how can you access it for free without running any ads. However, we will see how to set up ads in google ads for promoting our apps that are a part of digital marketing later in this book.

Something like this happens when you try to access google keyword planner without setting up ads.

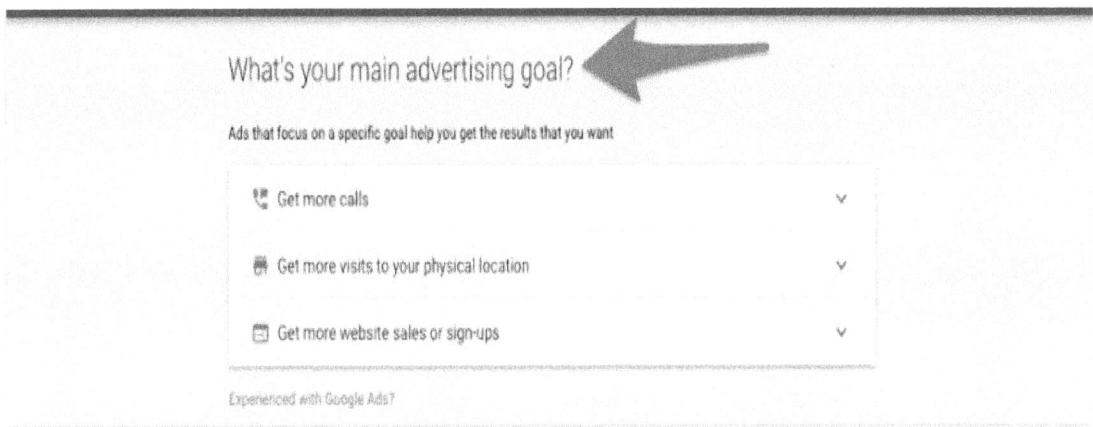

1. Click on Experienced with Google ads.

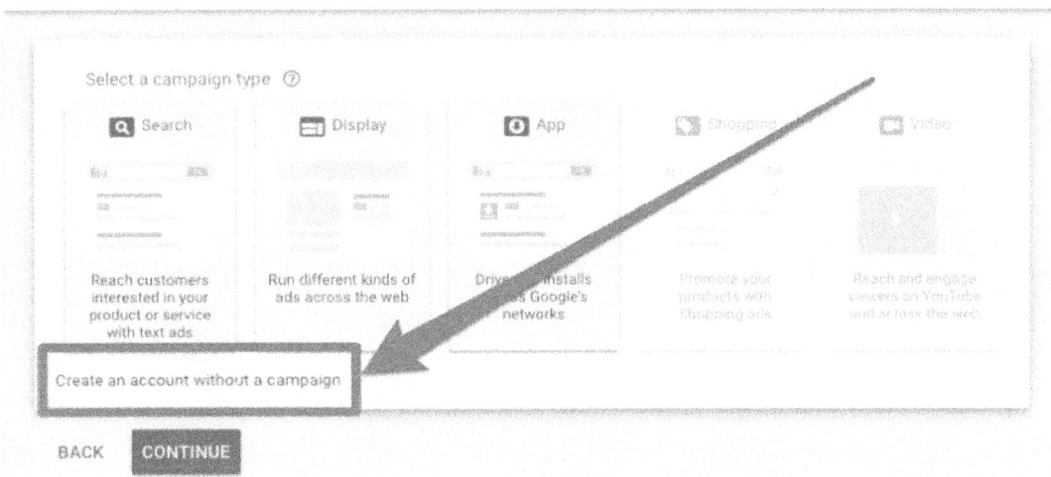

2. Click on Create a account without a campaign.

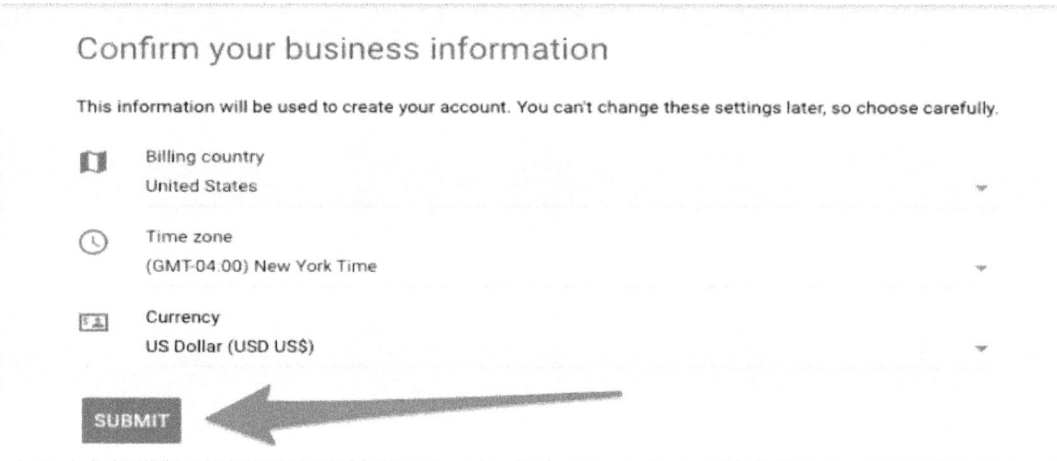

3.Click on submit button .

Don't worry no money will be deducted from your account.

4.Click on explore your account and your are ready to go.

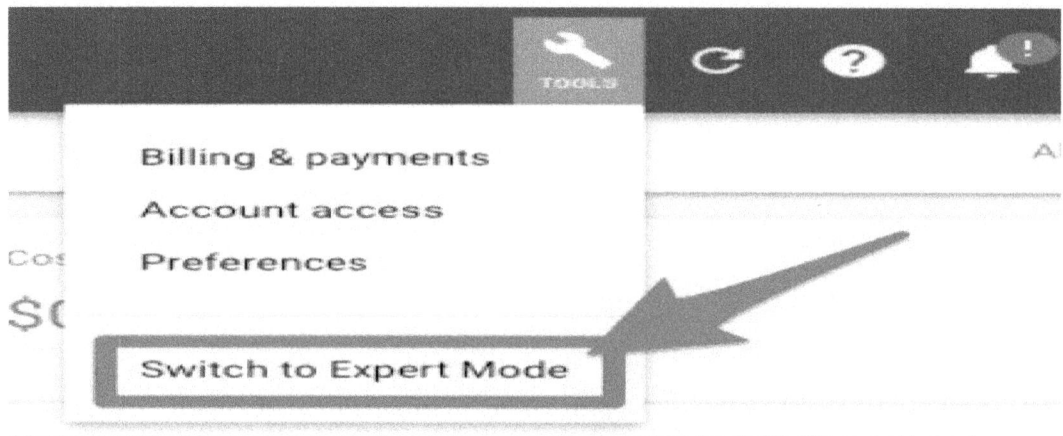

5.Futher click on tools and activate Switch to Expert Mode.

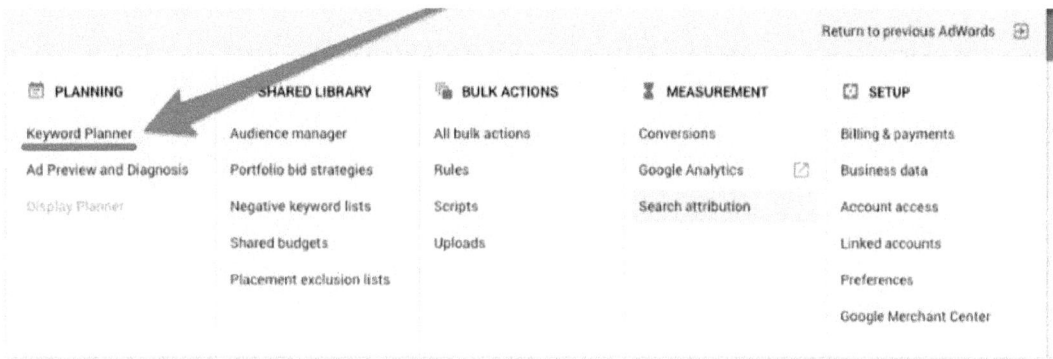

6.Further click once again on tools and click on keyword planner.

Now you are completely ready to go.

How to Use Google Keyword Planner.

Google keywords planner has two options to get started,

1.Find Keywords - Get keyword ideas in detail.

2.Get search volume and forecast - See search volume and other historical metrics for your keywords and forecasts as well for how they might perform in the future.

1.Find keywords.

Just type in some keywords you want to know about, you have to use commas to separate keywords. You can use as many keywords you want to know about. See the below screenshot.

Here I have searched for the keyword "Love Quotes".

You can also check keywords that are related to keyword 'love quotes', we often call them supporting keywords that you may use it with your main keyword. Here the main keyword is 'love quotes' and rest keyword suggestions are supporting keywords.

For each keyword, you'll see:

Avg. monthly searches;

Competition;

Top of page bid (low range);

Top of page bid (high range)

Here in the above keyword, the average monthly search of keyword "love quotes" is 1M TO 10M and competition is low. Low competition means less number of people are working for this keyword and there is less competition in it. Lesser the competition, the higher the chances of getting ranked. You can see that the traffic for this keyword is higher and the competition is low.

So you can go for developing an app on this keyword such as "Love quotes for her", Amazing love quotes, cute quotes, etc.

In the above keyword -

Type of page bid (high range)" shows the higher range of what advertisers have historically paid for a keyword's top of page bid, based on your location and Search Network settings. The average CPC of your keywords may vary. Type of page bid(low range) shows the minimum range of what advertisers have paid for a keyword.

Below is the example of doing a keyword search.

2. Get search volume and forecasts.

If you already have a list of keywords that you wish to see metrics for? Follow these steps.

Just paste the keywords in, hit "Get started," and it'll take you to the Forecasts section.

Keyword	Ad group	Max CPC	Clicks	Impressions	Cost	CTR	Avg. CPC
keyword research	Ad group 1	£0.28	2,996.99	27,944.03	£340.22	10.7%	£0.11
link building	Ad group 1	£0.28	279.36	6,452.10	£46.17	4.3%	£0.17
seo	Ad group 1	£0.28	13,384.69	200,259.50	£2,020.12	6.7%	£0.15

There are no keyword suggestions here. It shows how many clicks and impressions you can expect should you decide to run ads for your chosen keywords on Google AdWords over the next 30 days. You'll also see estimated costs, CTR, and CPC.

Most of this data is clearly aimed at AdWords advertisers. But here's a quick trick:

Go to the "**Historical Metrics**" tab and you will see 12-month average search volumes for your keywords. These are the same ranges you see when starting with the "Find new keywords" option.

Keyword	Avg. monthly searches	Competition
building link	10K – 100K	Low
keyword research	10K – 100K	Low
seo	100K – 1M	Low

Alternate - You can also use ahrefs keyword explorer, however, it provides 7 days trial currently and you have to pay after the trial ends but you will find it easier to do keyword research using ahrefs keyword planner

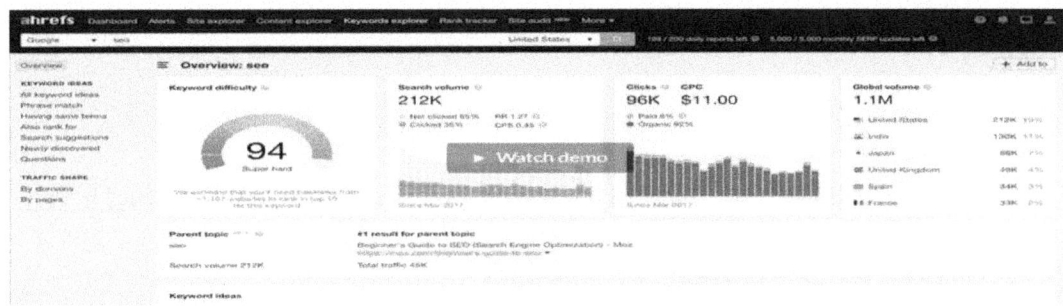

Above is the screenshot of ahrefs keyword planner. Apart from Google keywords planner, this planner is also regarded as one of the best keyword planners. The only difference between google keyword planner and ahrefs tools is that the former is free and the later is paid.

Chapter Nine

List Of Some High Traffic Low Competition Keywords

Some list of high traffic low competition keywords that might be helpful for you.

- **Love Quotes**
- **Good morning quotes**
- **Biography**
- **Hindi kahaniya**
- **Baby girl names**
- **Baby boy names**
- **Tree**

Category of Most Used Apps Right Now.

1. **Game Apps -** Game apps such as kids game.learning apps etc are higher in demand.

2. **Social and Photo Apps** - Social and photo apps such as pic editor,filter apps,birthday wishes maker apps,name maker apps etc are in great demand.

3.**Dating Apps -** These types of apps are getting more and more popular because of the modern demand and easy access to internet.The apps has higher engagements than any other apps and more app opens as well.People tend to stay more on these types of apps.Developing a dating app is a good idea.

How to Apps
How to apps are also in great demand.Creating a guide or a tutorial app can help users to know the subject better.How to apps are gaining popularity day by day.

3. All In One Apps
All in one apps are getting more and more downloads these days on app stores.All in one apps such as all in one food ordering app,all in one shopping app,all in one social media app etc can save a ton of storage space for users and are highly efficient as well.

CHAPTER TEN
MONITIZING YOUR APPS

Monetizing your application in the right manner is one of the most troublesome assignments in the mobile application business. Monetization in short can be defined as the way toward generating incomes from your application by either running advertisements or in-application purchases, affiliates, etc. The most common method of monetizing applications is showing advertisements. Google Admob owned by google(explained in subtleties later in this book) is probably the most ideal approach to monetize your app.However we need to make a rundown when we really need to monetize our application.

You can monetize your application from the initial day of its launch itself however it would not produce incomes with few downloads. It can possibly create good incomes if the application is getting at least 500-1000 downloads each day. You can monetize your application when the application really begins getting downloads and give your users an extraordinary experience at first without disturbing them with advertisements. However, this is optional. If you are running less as far as cash so you can definitely show advertisements from the first day itself to get back certain sums you would spend on Digital Marketing.

- Some Advertisement Networks.

- Google Admob

- Facebook Ads

- AppLovin

- StartApp

Should your Application be free or paid?

This is one of the most significant inquiries that is asked. People consistently go with the expectation of free stuff and not paid. However, there are numerous effective paid applications too. But at first, you can distribute your application as free with some in-application buys and make a paid application afterward subsequent to increasing some success that would be more ideal. It solely relies on you what cost you need to set on the off chance that you need to distribute your application as a paid app. The lowest price range for a paid app is around %0.99 to $1.99. However ASO that is Application store Optimisation works for free applications to get downloads from application stores organically through looked through keywords.

Making Money With Ads

To be perfectly honest speaking, no one enjoys advertisements, and on the off chance that you bombard your application with such a large amount of advertisements, at that point you are probably going to lose your user. So attempt to keep ads as least as conceivable that doesn't demolish users' experience with any cost. The incomes for the most part relies upon CPC that cost per click on advertisements and CPI that is the cost per thousand impressions. I Have discussed subtleties later in this book.

However, there are several kinds of ad formats that you can use for your apps.
- Banner Ads
- Interstitial Ads
- Native Ads and In content ads

Banner Advertisements - The easiest and most common kinds of ads are banner ads. These ads are rectangular advertisements set at the base of the screen. It mainly consists of text and image. However, the CTR that is Click Through Rate percentage of these advertisements is least then all other advertisement formats. The CTR of banner advertisements is for the most part 1% that is one user will click your ad out of 100 users which is least than all other advertisement formats. However, banner advertisements are the most well-known advertisements that are used by developers.

Interstitial Ads - These are full-screen advertisements that comes when users explore another action or activity of the app. In short, this is a pop-up ad. The CTR of these sorts of ads is most extreme and users will in general snap more on interstitial advertisements instead of banner ads or other advertisement formats. The CTR of interstitial ads is 4% to 5% which is substantially more than banner ads. In fact, it is most elevated among all other promotion formats. Keep the frequency of Interstitial ads as minimum as could be expected under the circumstances or it may aggravate the user and experience. Interstitial ads can be a blend of both text.images and videos advertisement.

Native Ads and in content advertisements - Native Ads are advertisements of fixed sizes set anyplace in the application according to the free space. The size of native ads is variable. You can pick the size that best accommodates your apps. In content, advertisements are the same as native ads that are put in the middle of content in your application.

Insights concerning CPC,CTR and so forth are clarified later in this book.

Making Money With Affiliates

Affiliate marketing has picked up tremoundous potential over the years. Affiliate marketing in short can be characterized as the way toward accepting a commission for promoting other products. You can procure commission once the sale is completed. There are part of affiliate suppliers, for example, Amazon, flipkart, bluehost and numerous more. When you promote items and the users finishes the sale, you gain a commission to a limit of 5%. You can utilize affiliate marketing methodology to create incomes inside your application.

For instance your application is about web hosting, then you can attempt to promote web hosting items as affiliates inside your application and make commission to it.

Making by selling your own items or products or Services.

You can sell your own items or services simply like an eCommerce app. You can sell your digital products, books, digital books, and ebooks, etc, and bring in money straightforwardly from your application without displaying any sorts of advertisements. You can likewise sell your services, for example, business coaching, development services, marketing, etc.

IN App Purchase

The best of making money from the app is in-app purchases. Try to figure out what your users really need. You can provide in-app purchases such as remove ads where users can remove ads permanently paying a certain price. You can add in-app purchases for buying subscriptions and man y more. You can reward certain credits to your users for a specific price in-app purchases. The list is countless.

Chapter Eleven

Top Money Making Apps

Here I have enlisted down some category of apps that will increase your chances of generating revenues from your app and are considered to be money-making apps.

1. Gaming Apps
2. Social Apps
3. Shopping Apps
4. Retail Apps
5. Scanner Apps
6. Communication Apps
7. Dating Apps
8. Task Apps
9. Lock Screen Apps
10. How to guide apps
11. All in one app
12. Picture editor apps
13. Surveys apps
14. Passive Income apps
15. Miscellaneous apps.

Chapter Twelve

What is Digtal Marketing and its types.

What is Digital Marketing?

According to Wikipedia Digital marketing is the component of marketing that utilizes the internet and online-based digital technologies such as desktop computers, mobile phones, and other digital media and platforms to promote products and services. Its development during the 1990s and 2000s changed the way brands and businesses use technology for marketing. As digital platforms became increasingly incorporated into marketing plans and everyday life, and as people increasingly use digital devices instead of visiting physical shops, digital marketing campaigns have become prevalent, employing combinations of search engine optimization (SEO), search engine marketing (SEM), content marketing, influencer marketing, content automation, campaign marketing, data-driven marketing, e-commerce marketing, social media marketing, social media optimization, e-mail direct marketing, display advertising, e-books, and optical disks and games have become commonplace. Digital marketing extends to non-Internet channels that provide digital media, such as television, mobile phones (SMS and MMS), callback, and on-hold mobile ring tones. The extension to non-Internet channels differentiates digital marketing from online marketing.

Types of Digital Marketing

- Search Engine Optimization (SEO)

- Search Engine Marketing and Pay-Per-Click Advertising
- Social Media Marketing
- Content Marketing
- Affiliate Marketing
- Influencer Marketing
- Email Marketing
- Mobile Phone Advertising

Chapter Thirteen

Types of Digital Marketing in Detail.

1. **Search Engine Optimisation(SEO)** - Search engine optimization or SEO can be defined as a set of rules that can be followed by website or blog owners to optimize their websites for search engines and thus improve their search engine rankings.

WHY SEO IS NEEDED FOR ANY BLOG OR WEBSITE.

Seo is needed for our blogs for a number of factors. Since in today's competitive market, Search engines serve millions of users per day looking for answers to their questions or for solutions to their problems.

So its a must for your blog that your blog should be visible to the users whenever they search for anything related to your keyword. Since there are millions of websites and blogs containing the same article what your blog has so it's not possible that whenever anyone searches for a particular keyword, your site would be displayed. within the first ten search results known as SERPs(Search Engine Page Rankings). For that, you have to do SEO that is to optimize your site and make it friendly to search engines so that your site ranking may be increased and would appear in the first page of search engines whenever anyone searches for keywords related to your blog or article.

Here are few of the factors why seo is important for your blog –

- ◉Most of the search engine users more often click on one of the top 5 suggestions in the results pages (SERPS), so to take advantage of this and gain visitors to your web site or blog you need to in the top positions.

- ◉Users trust search engines and having the presence of your blog in the top positions for the keywords the user is searching, increases the web site's trust.

TYPES OF SEO-
There are 2 types of SEO.

1- ON PAGE SEO

2- OFF PAGE SEO

ON PAGE SEO – On page seo is something that you do with your blogs or customise your blog to make it seo friendly.On page seo comes under all the seo techniques we utilize on our page to get our site ranked. Example includes title, meta tags, description, link structure, optimizing images, site speed, heading and sub headings and so on.

Here are some of the points how to do on page seo with your blog-

1. TITLE – Your title should be relevant and unique and should contain the keyword of the topic you are writing in your article. Make sure the title of your post is catchy and would compell the users to view the page.

2. DESCRIPTION – Give a suitable description or meta tag for your article. Don't repeat the title in the description. Keep the description short and don't use too many keywords.

3. PERMANENT LINK STRUCTURE – The permanent link structure is a term used to describe the format of URLS for pages (categories/tags) or individual posts of a web site.

It is shown in the browser address bar and in the search results (below the page title).

Make URL of your articles simple and easy to understand..

Use – to separate words.

Keep it short simple and descriptive.

4. DEVIDE YOUR BLOG POSTS IN CATEGORIES-

Your blog posts should be divided into categories. For example, if you are writing something on android devices, label it as android devices, and if something on pc so label it as pc and keep the categories at the top of your blog so that the user would find it easy to navigate.

5.INTERNAL LINKS – Redirect the user from one article of your blog to other article by including the links of other articles of your blog.Do this only when your one article is related to the other article of your blog..

6.TEXT FORMATTING – Use headings and sub headings and also paragraphs. Use bold and italics as well to attract users attention.

7.PAGE SPEED – Increase the page speed by removing unnecessary plugins and large sized images and javascript. Use tools that are available to analyse your pagespeed of your website.

The website that loads faster –

- Rank better in search results
- Get more page visits per user
- Get more conversions

8. ADD SITEMAP OF YOUR SITE ON SEARCH ENGINES - Add a sitemap of your website to google search console so that your website and posts are indexed by google.

OFF PAGE SEO –

Besides making changes to your website or blog to increase its search engines rankings you also need to do off page seo..
.

> *Off-site SEO is generally known as link building but it would be better to use the term web site promotion since a proper way to promote website involves much more methods and techniques than building links*

Here are some of the steps to do off page seo-

Make your website or blog as seo friendly so that the search engine robots would easily crawl your website. Use the tool known as SEMrush that will pick and tell you about all the issues that you should fix on your website to make it seo friendly.

Great Ways to Gain traffic to your website or blog or landing page.

1.GIVE ANSWERS ON QUORA..

I think no one would have written this before that quora can give traffic to a website or landing page. It definitely can. This is my personal experience. So what you have to do, just giving answers on quora won't gain you traffic. To find questions on quora of the topic you have already written on your blog or website or is related to your landing page and write some points in the answer and give the link of your article. This would gain you much traffic and if your content is good, the visitor will surely follow your blog or subscribe to your blog for sure and will visit again. Everyone knows content is king if you have great content for your blog. No one can stop your site to gain traffic. The same applies to the landing page as well.

2.BLOG COMMENTING

You can create backlinks of your blog and landing page by commenting on other websites articles and putting the link of your own blogs article at the end of the comment. You can do this time and time to one website to other.

3.WRITE GUEST POST AND ALSO HAVE A GUEST POST PAGE TO YOUR BLOG SO THAT OTHER CAN ALSO GUEST POST ON YOUR BLOG.

Guest post is something that can bring a huge amount of traffic to your blog. Also you should allow others to do guest post on your blog to give your blog more exposure.Guest post on websites that have good rankings and huge traffic and add a dofollow link of your blog. Doing guest post and also allowing guest post on your blog can increase your blogs traffic to great extent.This applies only to blogs and not landing pages.

4.GET IN TOUCH WITH SOCIAL MEDIA.

Share and promote your articles on social media such as facebook, twitter, linkedin, pintrest, google plus and many more. Create pages of your blog on these social media and place the link on your blog or landing page.

5.FORUM COMMENTING – Comment on forums that is related to your articles and landing page and give a link of your article in your comments.

5. **ARTICLE SUBMISSIONS-** Submit your articles to article submission sites.

Some of the article submission sites are –

- Goarticle.com
  Articledashboard.com
  Buzzle.com

Etc

This sites collect articles and allow a bio section that contains links to your blog.

2. Search Engine Marketing - Search Engine Marketing (SEM) includes running ads on various search engines such as Google, Yahoo and Bing, etc. Some of the examples are Google ads owned by google, bing ads,media.net, etc. These services such as google ads work on PPC that is pay per click, which means you have to pay only when the viewer clicks on your advertisements shown by these platforms such as google ads on their search engines.

3.Social Media Marketing(SMM)- Advertising on any of the social media platforms such as Facebook, Twitter, Instagram, LinkedIn, etc are known as social media marketing. For example, you have a post on Facebook where you are selling your ebook so you need to boost that post or in other words advertise that post to reach more audience that will ultimately higher your sales. This type of marketing is known as social media marketing.

4.Content Marketing - When you share a valuable piece of content online with marketing perspective either on your blog,website,youtube channel or a post ,or even a tweet on twitter,all comprises of content marketing.

5.Affiliate Marketing - Affiliate marketing is basically paying a commission to someone for conversions. You can take an example of amazon associates which is an affiliate marketing service provided by Amazon. When you sign up for amazon affiliates you get an affiliate link and if someone bought any product from that affiliate link, you earn a commission as decided by amazon. This is Affiliate marketing. You can also hire someone for your product sales and pay him commission for each product sale or conversion.

6.Influencer marketing - When you contact someone who has enormous reach and is widely known to people in short known as influencers for marketing your products. This is known as influencer marketing. It can be anyone such as a youtube channel with a very high amount of subscribers, a blogger, an Instagram star, etc.

7.Email Marketing - Email marketing refers to marketing your products to your email subscribers that you have earned either through your blog,website or youtube channel.In short they are your email subscribers.

8.Mobile Phone Advertising - This mainly includes mobile advertisement through SMS.

Chapter Fourteen

Some Killer ways to market your app.

1.GIVE ANSWERS ON QUORA..

Quora can bring amazing traffic to your app. This is my personal experience. So what you have to do, just giving answers on quora won't gain you traffic. To find questions on quora of the topic that is related to your app and write some points in the answer and give the link of your app and you can show some screenshots of your app too. This would gain you much traffic and if your content is good, the visitor will surely install your app.

2.Commenting

You can get installs on your app by commenting on other websites' articles and putting the link of your own app at the end of the comment. You can do this time and time to one website to another.

3.WRITE GUEST POST.

Guest post is something that can bring a huge amount of traffic to your blog. and also for your app. Guest post on websites that have good rankings and huge traffic and add a do-follow link to your app.

4.GET IN TOUCH WITH SOCIAL MEDIA.

Share and promote your app on social media such as Facebook, Twitter, LinkedIn, Pinterest, google plus, and many more using hashtags. Hash Tags will allow you to get more reach.

5. **Joining groups on facebook** -

Join groups on Facebook related to apps etc. Join groups that have more members and high engagement. Share your apps on that groups adding some valuable content. You can surely get in installs from there.

Chapter Fifteen

How to Save Marketing cost by monitizing our app with Admob.

How to monetize your app to save marketing costs.

Before we move on to the next chapter of digital marketing where we will learn how to set up campaigns on google ads and Facebook to promote your app. Before that, we should monetize our app with google AdMob so that we can save some marketing costs. We shall be showing ads on our apps to generate revenues.

One side we would be investing in our app promotion and on the other side, we will also generate revenues by showing ads on our apps so that we can reuse that generated revenue to remarket our apps.

Admob ads are the most commonly used ads for monetizing free apps. The basic idea is that we get revenue when the user clicks on any of the ads. The cost per click (CPC) depends upon various factors and on country to country.

Google Admob works the same way as Google Adsense. Both are Google products. The only difference is that google Admob is used for apps and AdSense is used for monetizing blogs and websites but the working process is the same. Although both have some different ad types.

Let's know about AdMob in detail -

WHAT IS GOOGLE ADMOB AND HOW DOES IT WORKS.

Google AdMob is one of the best advertising networks owned by Google. Google AdMob is an advertising network that pays money for showing ads on your apps and also for the person who clicks the ads shown on your app. Google Admob pays money for Cpc that is the cost per click, and also for 1000 ad impressions and page impressions. I will explain all the process of how do we get paid from Google AdMob. Now, let's know about what is CPC, rpm, etc etc in google Admob and what's the process, how it pays us, etc..

CPC – It is the cost per click that is AdSense will pay you if anyone clicks on your ads displayed on your app. CPC rates may vary from country to country. The US provides the highest CPC rates.

CPM – CPM means cost per 1000 impressions. Advertisers running CPM ads set their desired price per 1000 ads served and pay each time their ad appears. As a publisher, you'll earn revenue each time a CPM ad is served to your page and viewed by a user.

RPM- Rpm stands for revenue per 1000 ad impressions. So you will get paid when 1000 ads are displayed on your app. Before it was called ecpm.

Note – RPM is a reporting feature and this does not represent the actual amount paid to a publisher. For example, if a publisher earned $20 from 2,000 page impressions, thenRPM = (Estimated Earnings / Page Impressions) * 1000RPM = (20 / 2000) * 1000RPM = $10

RPM can be further classified into three types: Ad RPM, Page RPM, and Query RPM.

- **Ad RPM = (Estimated earnings / Ad impressions) * 1000**

- **Page RPM = (Estimated earnings / Number of page views) * 1000**

- **Query RPM = (Estimated earnings / Number of queries) * 1000**

You can know more about these on google Admob on its official website..

Chapter Sixteen

How To set up Google ads campaign for promoting your app.

In this chapter, we will see how can we set up google ads campaigns for promoting our app and getting in installs. In the previous chapter we have discussed how can we save our marketing cost and in this chapter we shall be discussing running promotions of our apps on different platforms mainly google ads and Facebook.

Lets get started.

Step 1 - Sign up for ads.google.com

Step 2 - Select manual payments instead of automatic payments.

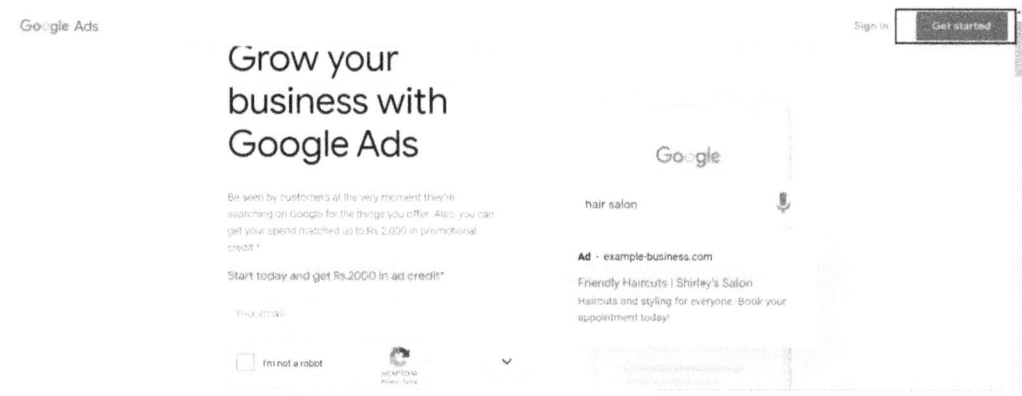

Step 3 - Below is the dashboard of google ads.

Click on the plus mark and add a campaign.

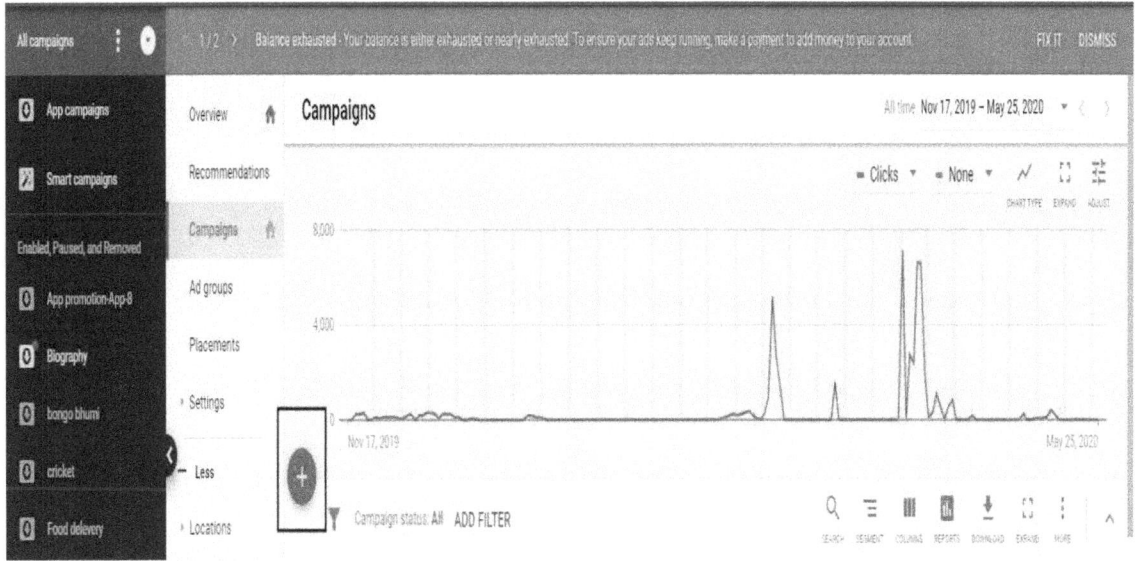

Step 4- Click on New Campaign

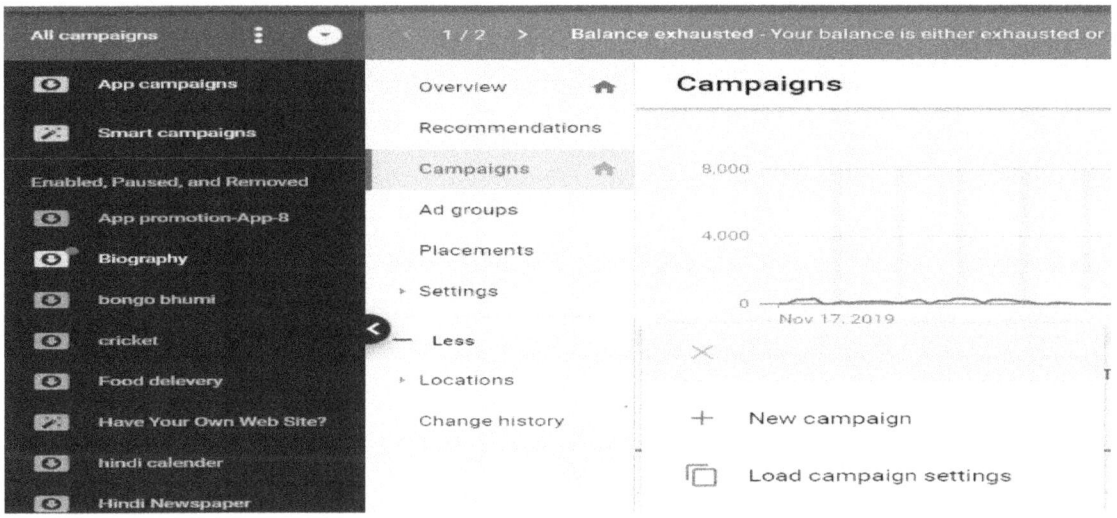

Step 5 - Select App promotion.

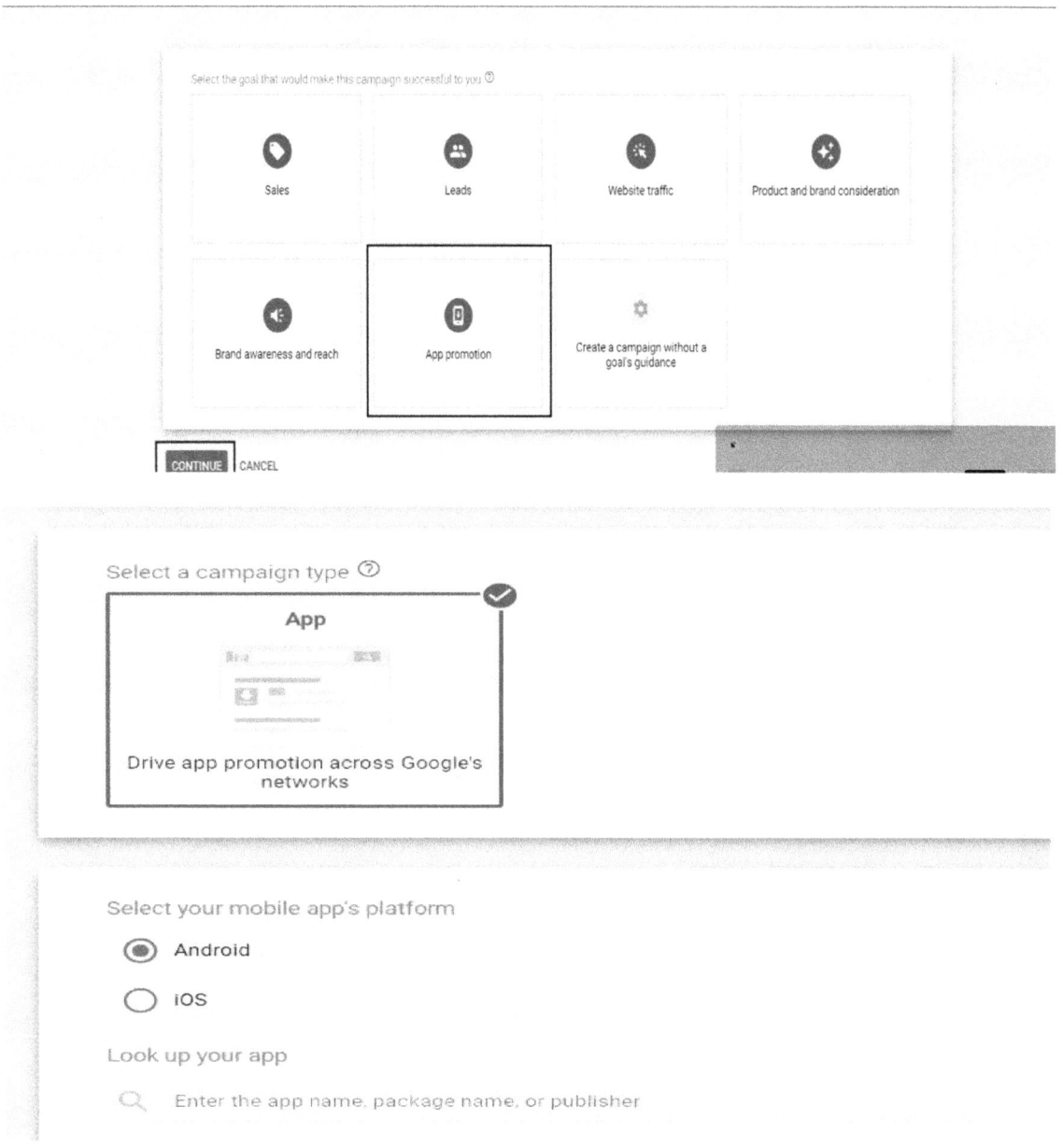

Step 6 - Select Android or IOS according to your prioroty.

Step 7 - Look up for your app in the search box either by typing the app name, package name or publishers name.

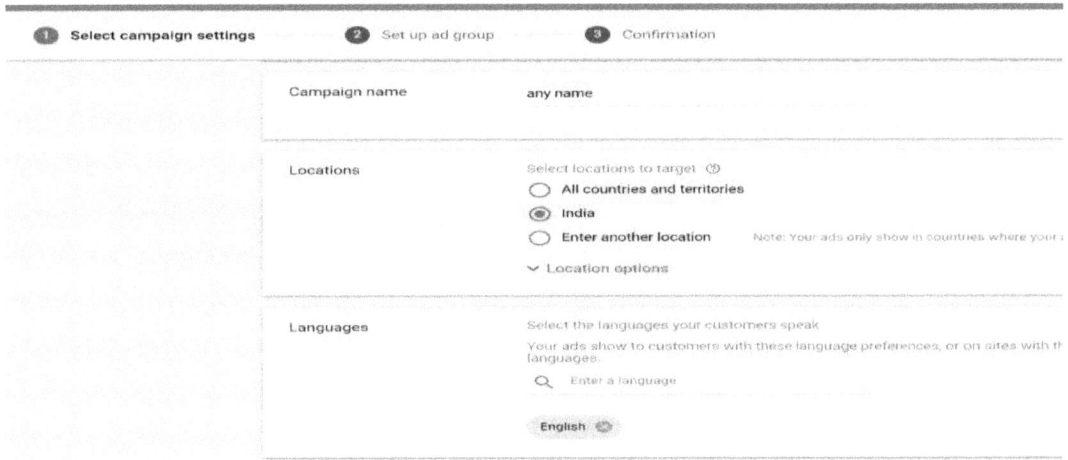

Step 8 - Give your campaign a name.

A name is becommes important when you are running so many campaigns as it helps you determine the performance of each campaign.

Step 9 - Select location.

Step 10 - Select language.

Please note this step is optional. By default language is english.

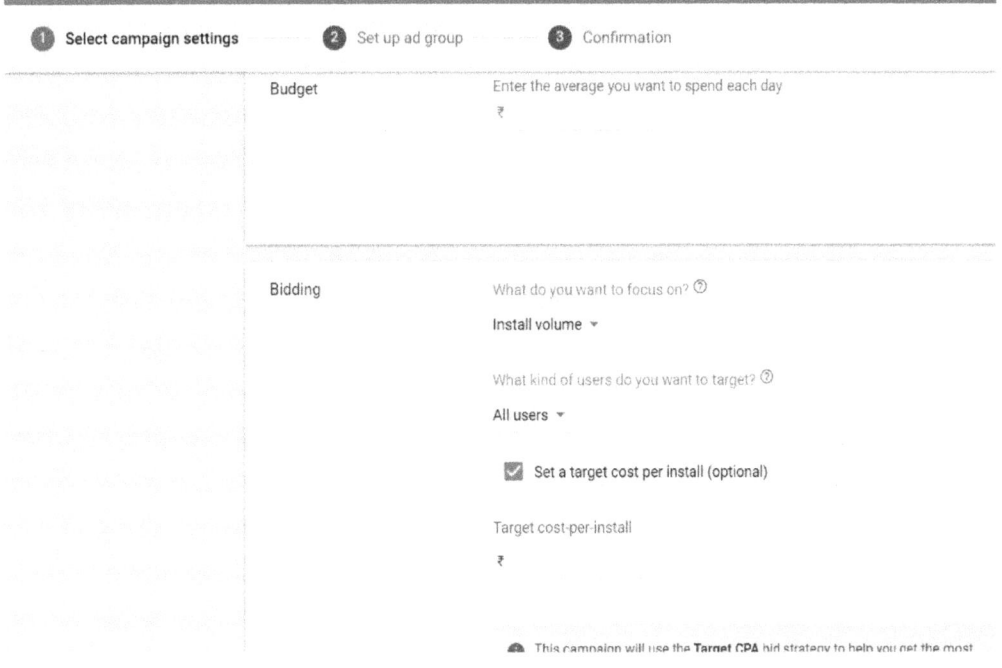

Step 11 - Select your budget for each day.

Recommendation is Rs 1000 per day as it will allow you to show more and more impressions and ultimately more installs.

Step 12 - Select Bidding amount.

You can choose Rs 2 here(as of India).Higher the bid more quickly you will get your app installs.It totally depends upon you how much you bid.If you bid too low,the ones who will bid higher will have higher priority and their ads will be shown firstly.

Target per installs means how much would you pay per one installs on your app.Here as mentioned Rs 2 will be paid for each app install.

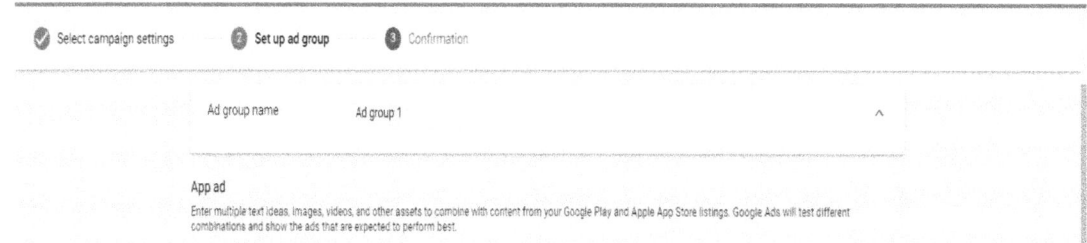

Step 13 - You can divide your campaign into different ad groups. It's only recommended when you want to run your campaign differently for different locations, audience, language, etc.

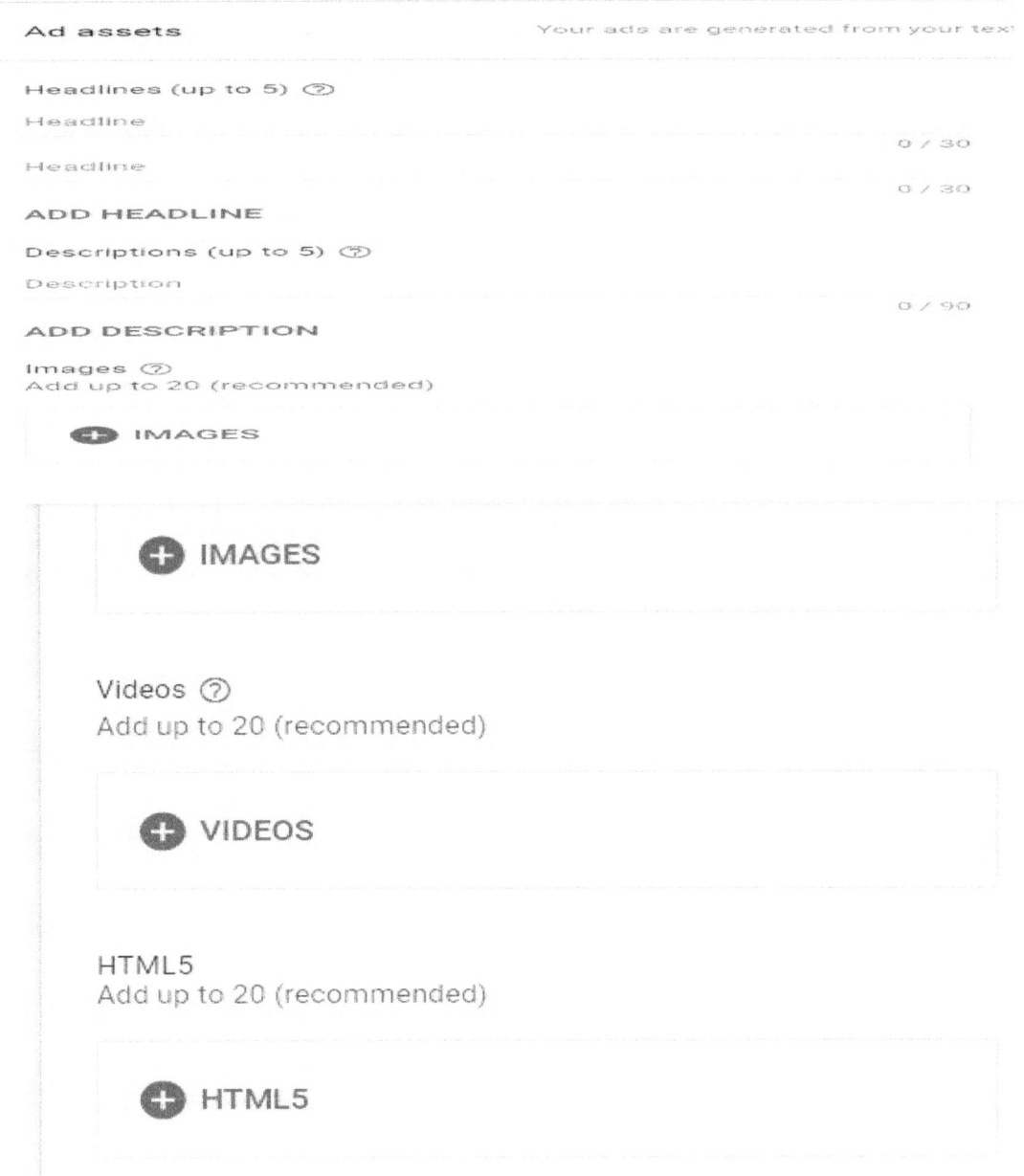

Step 14 - You can add headlines and descriptions for your app. It's suggested to put your app main keywords in headlines as well as descriptions.

Step 15 - You can add images and videos but its completely optional. If not you can skip this part.

This is how we run campaigns for our app promotion on google ads. After following all the steps wait for few hours to get your ad approved and your ad will be live and running. You can check all the information in your google ads dashboard.

Chapter Seventeen

How to set up ad campaign on facebook.

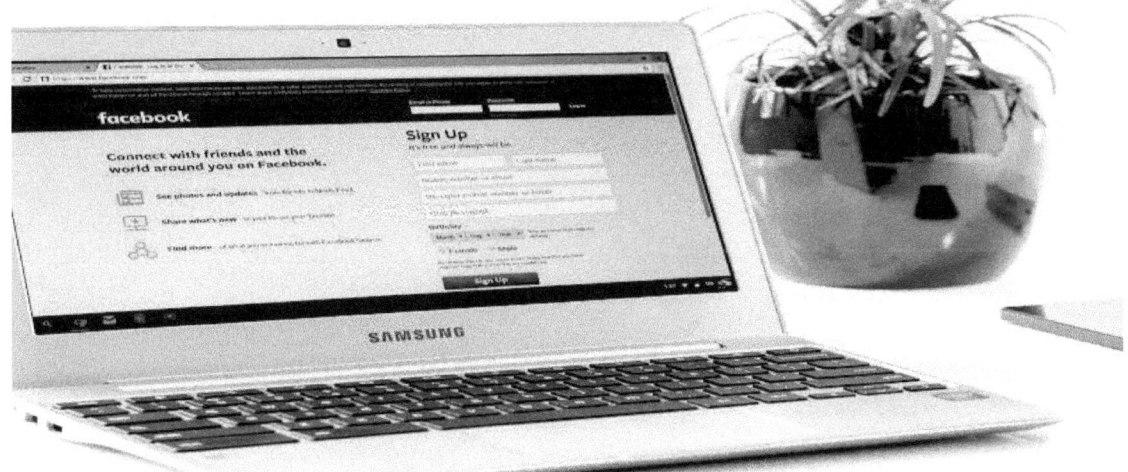

How to run a campaign on Facebook for app promotion.

With its humongous reach at 1.4 billion month to month clients all-inclusive, Facebook is one of the go-to places for entrepreneurs and advertisers while advancing anything. Whoever your objectives might be, odds are, they are on Facebook.

Steps to promote your app on facebook.

Step 1 - Create a page on facebook.

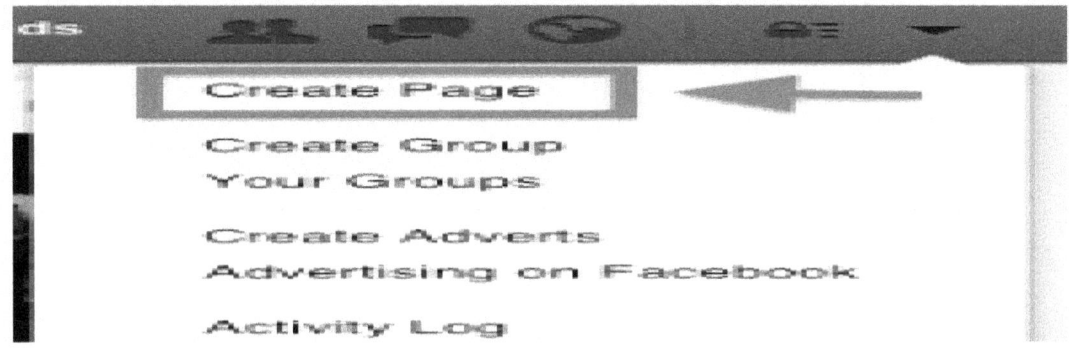

Step 2 - Click on the downward menu as shown in above image and click on create page.

Step 3 - You can select any of the options as per your priority but you are recommended to select the option brand or product which will further allow you to create a app page.

Note- Depending on the category you choose, facebook will ask you to fill up questions related to that particular category.

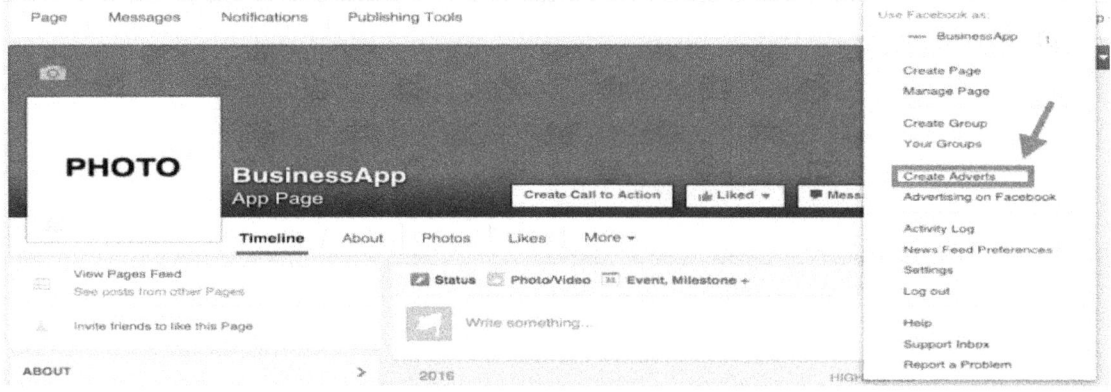

Step 4 - Create an advert account as shown in the above screenshot.

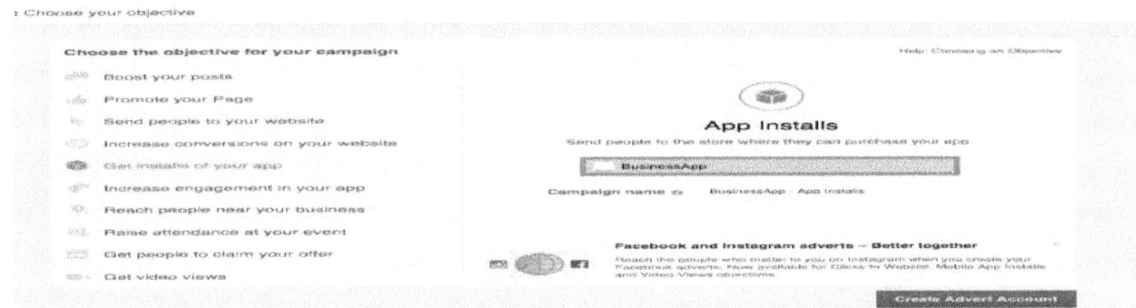

Step 5 - Select get installs of your app as shown above.

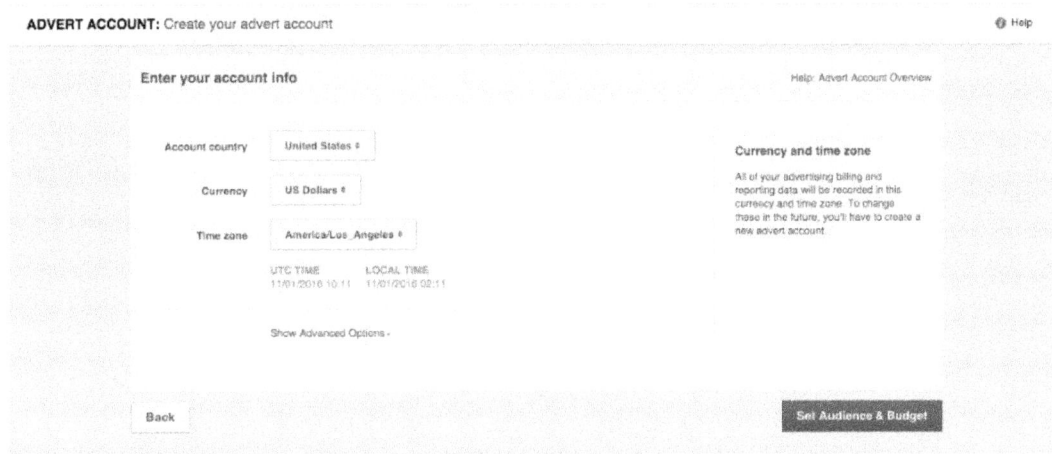

Step 6 - Select country, currency and time zone as shown in the above screenshot.

Step 7 - In this step you have to select your platform that is either android or ios, your target audience, age group and language.

Please note - If you app size is more than 100 mb or 200 mb, you are recommneded to choose wifi only over all mobile users in the section wireless connection.

Step 8 - Set your budget.

Set your bid amount. There are two options under bid amount. Automatic and manual. You can set up manual as shown in previous chapter or you can choose automatic bidding and let facebook manage your bidding automatically.

Step 9 - Select choose advert creative and select the ad options you get and you are ready to go. You have successfully created a app ad campaign on facebook.

Chapter Eighteen

How much installs do you really need for getting your app ranked in top 10.

That's an intense inquiry very as indicated by my own understanding, downloads anyplace between 1000 to 5000 are adequate for getting your application positioned at the top 10. I have an understanding of ranking more than 100+ applications remembering mine and my customers for the top inside 15 days by utilizing all the strategies referenced.

On the off chance that you are lacking in promoting you can at least attempt to get 1000 downloads by running application campaigns as referenced in past parts.

You have to get these installs when you launch your application since this is one of the key elements while ranking applications that what amount downloads your application gets inside first seven day stretch of its launch. So give earlier consideration to this and get the same number of downloads in the underlying days of your application launch and I promise you will discover your application getting positioned at top 10 inside 15 days.

After your application arrives at 10000 downloads, google will automatically begin prescribing or recommending your applications to users and you will begin getting increasingly more organic downloads from that point on.

Make sure to get as much as downloads within the first week of the app launch.

Chapter Nineteen

How to promote your app on quora without any investment.

WE all know that Quora is a place to gain and share knowledge. It's a platform to ask questions and connect with people who contribute unique insights and quality answers.

But do you know that we can also promote our app and gain some installs using quora.

Here are some of the steps you should follow to promote your app on quora -

1.Create a valuable content

2.Search questions related to your app.

3.Answer questions related to your app.

4.Add links of your app in your answers.

5.Add some screenshots of your app while writing an answer.

6.Write in such a way that your content provides value to the users.

Always focus on creating a valuable content that adds value to the viewers.You just can't share your app directly and tell them to download.No one will.Try to answer the question that is asked and then share your apps link.Your first priority should be adding valuable content then sharing your apps link.

Search questions that are trending or relates to the niche of your app and try to answer that question as mentioned above.

For example - If some one asked a question how can i reach 5000 downloads on my app easily.

So you should answer in a way that,

hey this is (your name),i uploaded an app on app store on (date) and applied certain ASO and marketing strategies to get 5000 downloads within 15 days.

The strategies were -

(mention your strategies and how you got those downloads)

This is one of my apps that reached 5000 downloads in 10 days.

(App link)+ screenshots(not more than 1).

Hope it helps.

The other way is that if some one asks which is the best app for watching live scores.

You can answer this way,

Hey there are several ways you can watch live scores but this is the best app that you can use to watch live cricket scores.

(some more content here)

(Your app link) + screenhsots.

This is how you can make full use of quora to market your app.However please note that quora has certain rules and regulations too,don't just share your apps link without adding any value to the questions asked.It may violate quora policies and your answer can be removed.

Chapter Twenty

How to promote your app on Facebook Groups.

As of December 2019, Facebook has over 250 million + monthly active users. Everyone knows the power of Facebook when it comes to marketing. You can do a paid promotion on Facebook as mentioned in previous chapters or you can make full use of Facebook groups to promote your app and gain installs.

Here are the steps you should follow -

1.Join a group with above 50K members in it atleast.

2.Join group that has more engagements(that is active members who like,comment and share).

3.Share your content .

4.Add links of your apps.

Firstly and foremost you have to join groups that have a minimum of 50k members in it. More the members, the more they reach your post will get. Also make sure that groups have engagements that are active members who like, share, and comment. The group should not be dead or is of no use to you. You can find engagements by joining the group if it is a closed group and by looking at the numbers of likes and comments a post is getting in that group.

Accordingly, you apply your marketing strategies.

You can use the same technique of providing content as mentioned in the previous chapter in the case of quora.

Chapter Twenty-One

How to promote your app by Commenting.

Yes, you heard it right, you can also promote your app by commenting. However, this is optional. You can use these techniques to gain some installs for your app.

You can comment anywhere providing some content and app link, it can either be a blog post, a website, a youtube channel video, a Facebook post, a twitter post, and so on.

Try to comment as much as possible, this might help you gain some installs to your app. Make sure you add value to the content and then share your link otherwise it may be considered as an spam. Your first priority while commenting should be adding value.

Chapter Twenty-Two

Paid Marketing

In this part, I will discuss paid marketing strategies to expand your application downloads and increase extra exposure. However, the ASO techniques I have referenced alongside Digital Marketing strategies are sufficient to get increasingly more downloads however we can likewise augment those downloads by and large by a portion of these paid advertising procedures.

These are some of the paid marketing Strategies.

1. Publicity and Press Coverage

2. Newspaper publications

3. Use your connections

4. Contact Bloggers and vloggers

5. Buy Ad space from websites.

Publicity and Press Coverage

Publicity and press coverage is something when your app gets featured in magazines, blogs, podcasts, youtube channels, tv and etc.

However getting published in magazines, youtube channels, blogs are not so easy but if you have higher marketing costs,you can always pay for getting published either on blogs, channels, or tv.

Newspapers Publications -

This mainly includes running your app advertisements in major newspapers. However, you have to pay certain price to show your ads in newspapers. The price may vary from newspaper to newspaper. This advertisement will surely give your app extra exposure which will ultimately bring a huge number of downloads at once.

Use Your connections

If you know someone with great people support and fan followers, you can definitely contact them to market your app.

Contact Bloggers and Vloggers

You can always contact top bloggers and vloggers for paid marketing. You can pay them a certain price to promote your app either on their blogs or on their youtube channels if they are vlogger.

Buy Adspace from websites

You can buy ad space from websites that have high traffic and pay a certain amount to them monthly to show your ads as sponsored ads. You can likewise do this for several websites.

CHAPTER Twenty-Three

MAXIMIZE DOWNLOADS OF ANDROID APP BY RELEASING IT ON MULTIPLE APP STORES.

On the off chance that you have an android application, you can go for releasing it on various application stores instead of publishing it just on google play store. There are a few other application stores too. By doing so your application will have more exposure to the audience and can get, increasingly more downloads from different application stores. Here is a rundown of all the application stores for android application.

- Google Play Store
- Samsung System Applications
- LG SmartWorld
- Huawei Application Store
- Sony Applications
- Amazon Appstore
- Aptoide
- F-Droid
- GetJar
- ACMarket
- SlideME
- Uptodown Market

- Itch.io
- Cydia
- neXva
- Bemodi
- AppBrain
- 1Mobile
- Appolicious
- Kongregate
- Appland

Chapter Twenty-Four

My DD business Model.

DD business model means Driving and Driven business models.I had nothing in my hand when I started my online business. I had no money for marketing Wats so ever. So I implemented a DD business model.

Driving and Driven business models mean a short term app will generate revenues and that revenues will be utilized for marketing long term apps.

Basically a driving app will drive your business and generate quick short time revenues and will drive other apps for marketing.

So I developed an app that was short term. I developed an app proving guide of a scheme/yojana implemented by Our prime minister of India. That scheme is valid only for 4 years. So I knew that this app could not be my long term business. But the keyword has amazing traffic and low competition with good CPC.So I published that app on play store, spent a few amounts of money on marketing and it was ranked in the top 10 applying good ASO strategies.

So that app started generating revenues and I utilized those revenues in my marketing my long term apps such as File Manager and Status downloader etc. This is how I started with my business applying DD business Model.

If you are too running short for money to spend in marketing, you can definitely use the DD business model to generate short term quick revenues that can be utilized later for marketing long term apps.

Chapter Twenty-Five

PPP Mindset.

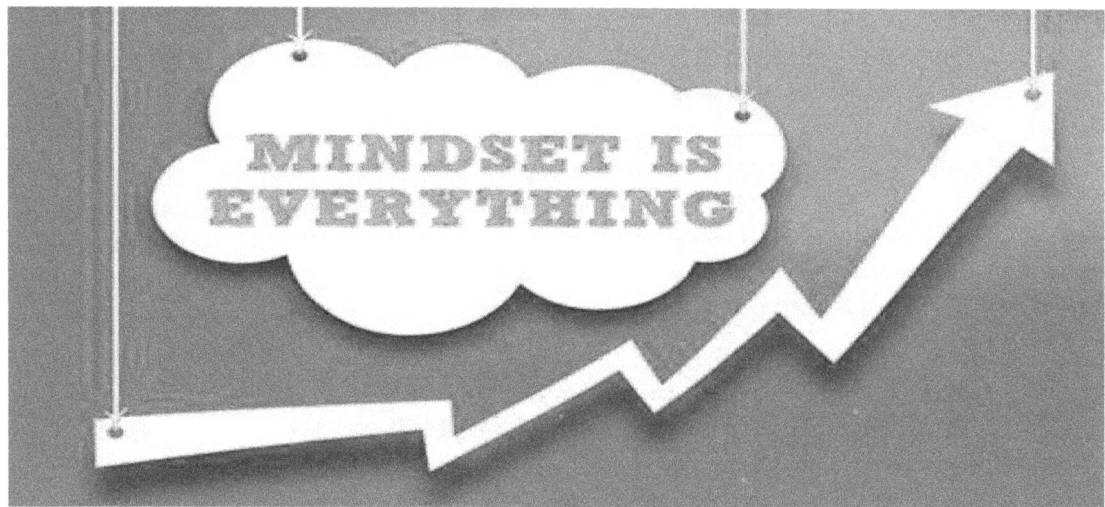

PPP Mindset is most important mindset you should have as an entreprenuer.

p _ Passion

P_ Patience

P_ Problem Solving

You should always have that belief and passion in you to achieve your goal no matter how hard the situation is.There will be situations that won't be your side but you have to deal with it.So passion is the first step to succeed.

The other is patience,90% of us just leave our work if we don't get desired results within few days and only 10% continue to do even with lot of failures,not even 10%,less than that and that few percentage of people are likely to succeed.So you should try to have ample patience.

Problem solving is one of the most important points one should have.We should be a great problem solver if we want to succeed.We have to look after the problems in the market and provide a solution to that problem and make others tasks easier ,the solution can be anything either in form of a app,website or anything.

PPP Mindset should be followed by each and everyone as an entreprenuer.

Be passionate,patient and great problem solver.

About the Author

Abhinav Ojha – Youngest App Marketing Expert In The World.

Abhinav Ojha who is 21 years old is the author of this book. Abhinav is one of the youngest app marketing experts in the world. You can search about him on google.

Abhinav has won numerous prizes for his aptitudes and presently he is the founder of Enterstor private limited.

Abhinav has been in online business since 2016. He has great love for technology. He is a passionate blogger. writer, poet, developer and an entreprenuer whose mission is to make people explore online oppurtunities which has gained tremendous potential over the years and make a living from online incomes.

He has worked for in excess of 6 organizations as a developer and digital marketing master and furthermore handles every one of his customers with a current team of 6 people.

Abhinav has helped more than 200 clients achieve their goals in the mobile app business.

Abhinav is an extremely enthusiastic dedicated boy who wants to have tea and espresso alongside playing some outside games, for example, cricket. Currently, he is infatuated with innovation.

Abhinav's Email Address - dabhinavojha@gmail.com

Facebook - https://www.facebook.com/abhinavojhaa

Thanking Everyone

Special Thanks to everyone for reading this book.Hope this book will add something to your success in Mobile App Business.

Dedication.

This book is dedicated to each and everyone who supported me and wished love for me and also believed in my potential.

Thank you all.

www.ingramcontent.com/pod-product-compliance
Lightning Source LLC
Chambersburg PA
CBHW041920180526
45172CB00013B/1343